OCCASIONAL PAPER 155

Fiscal Policy Issues During the Transition in Russia

Augusto Lopez-Claros and Sergei V. Alexashenko

INTERNATIONAL MONETARY FUND
Washington DC
March 1998

Cover design, charts, and composition:
Theodore F. Peters, Victor Barcelona, and IMF Graphics Section

Cataloging-in-Publication Data

Lopez-Claros, Augusto
   Fiscal policy issues during the transition in Russia / Augusto Lopez-
Claros and Sergei V. Alexashenko. — Washington, DC : International Mone-
tary Fund, [1998]

   p.   cm. — (Occasional paper ; ISSN 0251-6365 ; 155)
   ISBN 1-55775-703-8

   1. Fiscal policy — Russia (Federation).   2. Taxation — Russia (Federa-
tion) — Expenditures, public — Russia (Federation) — Russia (Federation)
— Social policy. I. Alexashenko, Sergei V. II. Title.
III. Series: Occasional paper (International Monetary Fund) ; no. 155.
HJ1211.52 .L26 1998

Price: US$18.00
(US$15.00 to full-time faculty members and
students at universities and colleges)

Please send orders to:
International Monetary Fund, Publication Services
700 19th Street, N.W., Washington, D.C. 20431, U.S.A.
Tel.: (202) 623-7430   Telefax: (202) 623-7201
E-mail: publications@imf.org
Internet: http://www.imf.org

recycled paper

Contents

CONTENTS

Figures Section

The following symbols have been used throughout this paper:

. . .   to indicate that data are not available;

n.a.   not applicable;

—   to indicate that the figure is zero or less than half the final digit shown, or that the item does not exist;

–   between years or months (e.g., 1994–95 or January–June) to indicate the years or months covered, including the beginning and ending years or months;

/   between years (e.g., 1994/95) to indicate a crop or fiscal (financial) year.

"Billion" means a thousand million.

Minor discrepancies between constituent figures and totals are due to rounding.

The term "country," as used in this paper, does not in all cases refer to a territorial entity that is a state as understood by international law and practice; the term also covers some territorial entities that are not states, but for which statistical data are maintained and provided internationally on a separate and independent basis.

Preface

Augusto Lopez-Claros is Senior Economist in the European II Department of the International Monetary Fund; he was Resident Representative of the IMF in Moscow during 1992–95. Sergei V. Alexashenko is First Deputy Governor of the Central Bank of Russia since December 1995. Between May 1993 and March 1995, he was Deputy Minister of Finance of the Russian Federation. The authors would like to thank Brian Aitken, Julian Berengaut, Odd Per Brekk, Daniel Citrin, Donal Donovan, Sanjeev Gupta, Robert Hagemann, Vincent Koen, Christopher Lane, Aleksei V. Mozhin, John Norregaard, John Odling-Smee, Carlos Silvani, and Thomas Wolf for their useful comments. In Moscow, Sergei M. Ignatiev, Andrei I. Kazmin, Sergei A.Vasiliev, Yevgenii G.Yasin, and Mikhail M. Zadornov provided key insights into various aspects of fiscal policy in Russia during the period under consideration. The authors remain solely responsible for the contents of the paper and their views do not necessarily reflect the views of the IMF or of the Central Bank of Russia. In the same spirit, expressions of gratitude to the above colleagues do not imply any responsibility on their part or of the institutions they represent. The authors are grateful to Esha Ray of the External Relations Department for her expert editorial contributions and for coordinating production of the publication and to Constance Strayer for her excellent assistance in managing the manuscript. In Moscow, Ksenya V. Maleeva provided able additional logistical support.

I Overview

Since 1992, the Russian Federation has moved away from a command economy and has laid the foundation of a market-based system. This paper examines some of the key policy issues that arose in the fiscal area in 1992–96, the period following the onset of economic liberalization and reform. The paper is organized as a series of largely self-contained pieces dealing, respectively, with revenue, expenditure, and social protection issues. The next section discusses the role of fiscal policy in the context of the Soviet plans and assesses some of the underlying rigidities that contributed to precipitating the difficult economic situation that characterized the late 1980s and early 1990s. Some of the early attempts at reform are also noted, as are the reasons for the emergence of sizable macroeconomic imbalances during that period.

In examining the role of fiscal policy during the transition period, Section III focuses initially on the factors contributing to the decline in revenues. The discussion highlights both the role of those elements inherent to the transition and those involving a discretionary policy component; in this latter regard, the roles of tax policy and tax administration are analyzed, with particular reference to the kinds of specific reforms that are needed to improve the efficiency of the tax system and to safeguard the revenue base. The main tax exemptions in terms of the associated forgone revenue are listed in an appendix.

The deterioration of revenues in Russia has imposed a sharp compression of government expenditure; Section IV identifies some of the relevant expenditure issues, including the appropriateness of coverage and aspects of its composition, the scope for additional expenditure compression over the medium term, and, because of the central role they play in the implementation of fiscal policy, budget formulation and execution and, more generally, fiscal management. The discussion on the budget process, in particular, is an attempt to present an "insider's" view of expenditure management and control as practiced in Russia during the initial period of the transition. Since much of Russia's social spending takes place on the margins of the budget, through various social funds, the issue of the efficiency of social spending remains very relevant to any discussion of the role of the government in furthering the cause of economic reform. Section V discusses social conditions and social protection in Russia, with special reference to the underlying weaknesses in the administration of social benefits, and the various policy reforms that are needed to make the system more responsive to the country's social needs. A final section presents a summary of the main policy recommendations.

II The Context for the Implementation of Fiscal Policy

The chief characteristics of a centrally planned economy began to emerge in the Soviet Union toward the end of the 1920s and early 1930s and eventually consisted of state ownership of the means of production; detailed quantitative central plans for enterprise inputs and outputs and for foreign trade and financial plans that reflected the physical flows of the plans; bureaucratic bargaining over access to resources in the context of the plan's targets; fixed prices, mainly to ease the planning process; and the fulfillment of the plan as the main criteria of enterprise efficiency. Other features included a "monobank" banking system and the separation of the money stocks of enterprises and households.[1] Two aspects of the centrally planned economy had a bearing on the nature of the fiscal system: the emergence of a level and structure of prices completely out of line with world levels and relativities and an exceptionally complex mechanism for the creation and redistribution of profits within the economy.

Background

Against this background the government's approach to the enterprise sector depended on a number of factors, including perceptions of the particular enterprise's profit potential. That different enterprises had different "surplus" potential called for the creation of a system of enterprise-specific financial planning with a view to ensuring a "desirable" redistribution of resources as well as the generation of an adequate level of state budget revenues.[2] In many respects, the fact that the number of independent production units was relatively small and the enterprises correspondingly large facilitated the functioning of this system, and campaigns were often launched to make enterprises even larger. Various types of producer associations were established to encourage the concentration of management and reduce the number of installations that needed to be run by the government. Financial and efficiency objectives were seldom, if ever, central to these attempts at concentration, which seemed more driven by a desire to keep the planning process manageable. Loss-making enterprises (to the extent that the notion of "loss" in such a system was well defined) were not, as a rule, closed down but the losses were instead absorbed by the state budget, through credits and subsidies extended by ministries.

The Gosplan (the State Planning Committee of the U.S.S.R.) was the center of the command economy, with responsibility for the formulation of a set of interrelated plans. These plans were prepared on a balance sheet format and were simply called "balances" and consisted essentially of comprehensive attempts at identifying sources and uses of resources. For instance, the "production and allocation balance" would identify in terms of physical units of output all sources of production and consumption in the economy. Similar balances were elaborated for investment, foreign trade, household incomes and expenditure, and the banking system. Because virtually the entire economy was state owned, there was, in principle, little distinction between financing of the budget and financing of all the economy. The state's general financial balance attempted to integrate the information contained in all sectoral balances in a way that would permit a decision to be made concerning what share of total financing would be carried out through the budget itself, and what shares through the sectoral ministries and the enterprises themselves. The general financial balance was the principal instrument of financial planning in the Soviet Union during the postwar period and formed the basis for the budgetary process.

The planning process was two-pronged. Enterprises drafted their plans, which were then revised by the industrial ministries, which in turn received "control figures" as plan targets from Gosplan. In its calculations, Gosplan specified primary targets in terms of the physical volume of production, and it manipulated prices, subsidies, wages, investment,

---

[1]For a comprehensive overview, see Wolf (1985).

[2]The very notion of a "state budget" was to a large extent arbitrary as it did not incorporate various articles of spending under the control of the state; since there was no other term, this term was used, inaccurately and misleadingly, to mean aggregate spending by the state.

and credit to redistribute resources among enterprises. Fiscal policy was passive, playing a subordinate role to other objectives (for example, output and the level of social spending), with the state budget being essentially the mechanism to effect such redistribution.

Government control over the activity of enterprises was mainly exercised through sectoral ministries that were fully responsible for the situation in their respective branches. All sectoral ministries received directives from the Gosplan and the Ministry of Finance concerning the amount of resources that their respective branches were compelled to channel to the budget. The ministries endorsed the financial plans of the enterprises subordinated to them and adopted decisions on spending by each of the enterprises. The sectoral ministries were instructed to find ways of redistributing financial resources of the enterprises under their jurisdiction in a manner that would ensure the normal development of production, the financing of expenditures for the maintenance of the social infrastructure that were listed on the balance sheet of enterprises (mainly social benefits and services), and their contribution to the state budget of those amounts requested by the Ministry of Finance and the Gosplan. The ministries were also responsible for accumulating financial resources needed for the implementation of major investment and research programs in the branch.

The guidelines for channeling profits and depreciation allowances to the sectoral ministry fund or to the state budget varied from enterprise to enterprise and from year to year, fluctuating between zero and 100 percent. Each enterprise's five-year plan was formally approved within the framework of the country's overall five-year plan,[3] but these intermediate financial plans were, as a rule, preliminary and were subject to respecification before the beginning of every calendar year. In fact, most financial plan indicators were revised throughout the year, sometimes up to the very end. The ministries also had to ensure the repayment of the losses made by the loss-making enterprises in the branch, if such losses could not be attributed to faulty decision making at a higher level of the management chain. In order to fulfill these and many other functions, the sectoral ministries were granted all the necessary legal rights to manage the financial resources of the enterprises subordinated to them.

The financial resources of enterprises available for redistribution included not only profits arising from production but also depreciation allowances intended for the renovation of fixed assets and for maintenance of the capital stock. The rate of depreciation allowance was set by the Gosplan and revised about once every ten years concurrently with a reassessment of the value of fixed assets, as was the case in 1973, 1982, and 1991. It is necessary to emphasize that, in principle, the entire volume of financial resources of the enterprises was subject to centralized management regardless of whether these resources were channeled to the budget or remained on the accounts of the enterprises; ad hoc direct intervention in the finances of individual enterprises to "correct" anomalies was quite common. Often the working capital of the enterprises was also partially redistributed within the branch.

Setting the Stage for Reform

In elaborating the financial plans for a given enterprise, the ministry assumed fixed prices for all inputs and output, although it was admitted that certain enterprises might be unable to contribute to the budget or, worse, might need financial support from the state. In such a case, the ministry was responsible for determining the volume of subsidies to be received by the enterprise and to agree for this support with higher authorities. As part of the plan, no account was taken of the potential information content of prices, and price stability (that is, fixity) was sought as much for the desirability of a stable purchasing power for the population as to facilitate the planning process itself. That fixed prices led to shortages or to growing "black" markets where prices were often several times higher than official levels was seen as a temporary maladjustment that needed to be understood (and dealt with, often) against the complexities of managing a plan that attempted to balance production, stock building, and the utilization of thousands of inputs to fulfill the primary objectives of the plan. Within this structure, price formation was difficult, with the preferred approach being the setting of wholesale prices at average cost plus a percentage markup. While this prevented "excessive" profits, it did not especially encourage cost savings, and, in time, the Soviet Union became one of the most inefficient and wasteful users of resources (such as electricity, energy, and labor), using more inputs per unit of output than in other industrial countries.

The interrelated system of fixed prices, intrasectoral and intersectoral reallocation of financial resources, and subsidization became the cornerstone of the Soviet economy and the basis of the budget. In time, although its rigidity came to be increasingly recognized, attempts at reform were made difficult by the realization that it would be very difficult to "improve" one element within the system while

---

[3]The financial plan not only endorsed the allocation of the financial resources of the enterprises but provided for a more complex process of coordinating prices, subsidies, and centralized investment distributed among the enterprises in the sector and among different sectors.

leaving the rest unchanged. For instance, in 1987 a Law on State Enterprises was adopted with the intention of promoting decentralization and giving enterprises greater managerial independence and autonomy concerning investment decisions, wage policy, utilization of profits, and so on. The main consequence of the policy, however, appears to have been the rapid growth of wages, the concomitant shortages, and a fairly extensive process of state asset expropriations by the increasingly autonomous managers, without any measurable improvements in efficiency, quality, or even physical output. Other measures adopted at various times aimed at "tightening labor discipline," reducing the energy intensity of production, and better directing investment to foster retooling and modernization of the industrial sector and improving the quality of output were of limited success, given the system's overriding need to fulfill production targets within a reasonably consistent matrix of inputs and outputs. While this period also witnessed some of the first manifestations of "glasnost," perceptions of continued drops in living standards also led to widespread public frustration and disappointment.

In parallel to what could otherwise be described as half-hearted, piecemeal (and at times inconsistent) attempts at reform, the macroeconomic climate in the Soviet Union worsened in the second half of the 1980s and in 1990–91. Fiscal pressures emerged on a number of fronts. On the revenue side, under the greater autonomy conferred to enterprises by the 1987 Law on State Enterprises, profit transfers remitted to the budget fell. Declining oil production and world market prices for energy (especially intense in 1986) also had a negative effect on budgetary revenues. Although prompted by legitimate public health concerns, the antialcohol campaign launched in 1985 sharply reduced turnover tax receipts.[4] On the expenditure side, the government raised procurement prices on agricultural products a number of times without concomitant increases in retail prices, leading to automatic upward adjustments in budgetary subsidies. Cleanup costs in the aftermath of the Chernobyl disaster in 1986 and social and humanitarian assistance following the earthquake in Armenia in 1988, together with periodic increases in pensions and other components of social expenditure, all contributed to a significant widening of the fiscal deficit. In addition, a tug-of-war began in 1990 between the Russian Federation government and the Union government (U.S.S.R.) to establish jurisdiction and fiscal control over the enterprise sector. The chief weapons in this process were the promise of lower tax rates for enterprises that switched allegiance, more generous subsidies, and, by 1991, Central Bank of Russia credits on highly favorable terms. By the spring of 1991, the bulk of Union enterprises located on Russian Federation territory had been reclassified as "Russian."

At the end of 1991, the fiscal deficit had set new records (close to 30 percent of GDP), the bulk of it financed by monetary emission, leading to a sharp rise in the ratio of M2 to GDP, to well over 70 percent.[5] At the same time, the rapid growth of real wages had led to strong demand pressures that, in the context of fixed prices, intensified shortages and the proverbial long lines. The fall in export revenues associated with lower oil production, the collapse of trading arrangements among member countries of the Council for Mutual Economic Assistance (CMEA), the rapid expansion of external debt during the second half of the 1980s, and the utilization of virtually the entire stock of foreign exchange reserves precipitated a balance of payments crisis characterized by growing external payments arrears, a drying up of loan disbursements, and a sharp contraction of imports and output.[6] A point worth making is that a (perhaps unintended) consequence of the battle for control of the enterprise sector was the creation of an environment in which the discretionary granting of tax concessions came to be perceived as a legitimate means to achieve other ends (for example, in 1991, political support) and enterprises were made to see clearly the benefits of lobbying the government for various forms of financial support. Akin to a soft budget constraint, the early establishment of such patterns of behavior may have had a direct bearing on Russia's subsequent attempts at financial stabilization (see Section III).

Price liberalization in early 1992 effectively permanently disabled the command structure at the basis of the planned economy and made it possible, at least in theory, to move quickly to a decentralized system of prices that would reflect relative scarcities in the marketplace. However, the initial assumption that free prices and the concomitant elimination of subsidies, together with large cuts in public investment and defense and increased revenues associated with the introduction of a value-added tax (VAT), would rapidly lead to budget balance in the course of 1992 proved unduly optimistic. Key prices in the economy were not lib-

---

[4] Tax revenue from alcohol products amounted to some 20 percent of total tax revenue.

[5] See Koen and Phillips (1993).

[6] For a detailed discussion of growing Soviet economic problems in the late 1980s, see the three-volume *A Study of the Soviet Economy,* 1991, jointly published by the International Monetary Fund, the World Bank, the Organization for Economic Cooperation and Development (OECD), and the European Bank for Reconstruction and Development. The main elements of this external crisis are also presented in Christensen (1994).

eralized fully (for example, energy),[7] thereby depriving the budget of an important source of revenue. The authorities and other observers of the Russian economy underestimated the magnitude of subsidization as well as the extent to which such subsidization, inefficient as it was, had come to acquire social protection elements. Perhaps more important, the authorities' stabilization objectives were undermined by the lack of broad-based support for the reform strategy, particularly at the enterprise level. By the spring of 1992, important concessions began to be made to enterprise managers and regions (for example, Northern Territo-

ries), mainly in the form of subsidized credits to agriculture and industry as well as by a general slowdown in the pace of structural reform in other areas. Contrary to initial expectations, far from achieving budget balance, the consolidated budget deficit in 1992, including many quasi-fiscal operations of the central bank incorporated into the budget during 1993–95, was probably well in excess of 50 percent of GDP,[8] the monthly rate of inflation soared to close to 30 percent in the last quarter of 1992, making the subsequent task of financial stabilization considerably harder than had been anticipated at the outset of the reforms.

---

[7]Because of the existence of export quotas on crude oil, effective price liberalization for oil did not take place until 1995.

[8]On some of the problems associated with measures of the fiscal deficit during this period, see Section IV.

III Priorities for the Modernization of the Tax System

Like other countries undergoing systemic transformation, Russia has experienced a radical contraction in the scale of the public sector as well as fundamental changes in the role of the state in the economy. A key element of the transition has been the move from an economy characterized by a "hyperactive state which sought to control all activity in society" (Kornai, 1992, p. 5) to one in which, increasingly, production and employment are being generated by a rapidly emerging private sector and in which the public sector no longer has the preponderant role as the chief intermediary of economic activity.

Factors Underlying the Decline in Revenues

The sharp contraction of revenues observed in virtually all economies in transition in Central and Eastern Europe has also manifested itself in Russia. As shown in Table 1, federal tax revenues in relation to GDP fell from 16.6 percent in 1992 to 11.9 percent in 1996.[9] Although the decline in local government cash revenues was not as pronounced, total revenue nevertheless fell from 28.4 percent of GDP in 1992 to 24.8 percent in 1995 and to some 23½ percent of GDP in 1996 (Figure 1). Given the sharp drop in real output, the drop in revenues is even more pronounced when measured in real terms.

Many of the same forces that led to the erosion of revenues in other countries in the region have also been at play in Russia. During 1991–96, Russia suffered a cumulative output decline of 42 percent, one of the largest in the region, and this decline had the expected impact on revenue (Table 2 and Figure 2). In the past several years, the Russian economy and, in particular, its industrial sector have been exposed to supply and demand shocks on a scale that may have no precedent in recent economic history (Table 3 and Figure 3). On the demand side, the emergence of a new political climate for international relations in the late 1980s led to

a major crisis in the military-industrial sector and a permanent drop in the purchases of military hardware and other defense-related equipment through the budget, as well as to reductions in capital spending. Given the magnitude of the industrial sector in the former Soviet Union (as late as 1990, over 50 percent of output originated in industry) and the prominence of military production within it, this demand shock was proportionally far more severe in Russia than the one that affected defense output elsewhere in the industrial world. The magnitude of this demand shift may be gleaned from one key indicator: arms exports by the Soviet Union, financed mainly through export credits to developing countries, fell from $20 billion in 1988 to less than $3 billion by 1992. In the military sector during 1992–93, cumulative output declined by 57 percent, and employment dropped by 51 percent.

Price liberalization and the move to a more transparent system of resource allocation also resulted in significant supply shocks, as the enterprise sector was gradually deprived of producer subsidies, foreign exchange at highly appreciated exchange rates, and raw materials—particularly energy—at a fraction of the world price. The easy access to credit on preferential terms was also phased out. The military sector, which during the Soviet era had been largely exempt from paying taxes as a way of enhancing its competitiveness, gradually began to be taxed. Consumer and producer subsidies (budgeted and unbudgeted and including subsidies on imports; see Section IV), which amounted to nearly 23 percent of GDP in 1992, were also drastically cut, thus adversely affecting household demand for goods.[10] Reforms in Eastern Europe—including external liberalization—resulted in sharp cutbacks in Soviet exports to traditional export markets, and declining oil production further undermined output growth.[11] The collapse in trade among members of the CMEA in

---

[9]However, over 3 percentage points of revenue in 1996 was collected in various forms other than cash.

[10]Consumer subsidies in Russia were embodied in the prices of hundreds of commodities, including basic foodstuffs, energy and fuel, children's clothing, and pharmaceuticals.

[11]Oil exports from Russia to countries outside the former Soviet Union fell from $27 billion in 1990 to $12 billion in 1992, a drop that largely reflects a contraction of volumes.

Table 1. Total Tax Revenue
(In percent of GDP)

	1992	1993	1994	1995	1996
Tax revenue[1]	28.4	27.8	25.7	24.8	23.7
Federal	16.6	13.7	11.8[2]	12.1[3]	11.9[4]
Local[5]	11.8	14.1	13.9	12.7	11.9
Of which:					
Profit tax	8.5	10.2	8.0	7.1	4.3
Federal	3.4	3.2	2.8	2.5	1.5
Local	5.1	7.0	5.2	4.6	2.8
VAT	10.4	6.7	7.0	6.5	6.9
Federal	7.8	4.3	5.1	4.5	5.1
Local	2.6	2.4	1.9	2.0	1.8
Personal income	2.3	2.6	2.8	2.2	2.5
Federal	—	—	—	0.2	0.2
Local	2.3	2.6	2.8	2.0	2.3
Excises	1.4	1.2	1.2	1.5	2.7
Federal	0.8	0.7	0.7	1.1	2.3
Local	0.6	0.5	0.5	0.4	0.4
Property	—	—	0.8	1.0	1.6
Federal	—	—	—	—	—
Local	—	—	0.8	1.0	1.6
Export and import duties	1.8	1.1	0.9	1.5	1.0
Federal	1.8	1.1	0.9	1.5	1.0
Local	—	—	—	—	—
Memorandum items:					
Total cash tax revenue					
(in percent of GDP)	28.4	27.8	25.3	23.0	20.6
GDP (in trillions of rubles)	18	172	611	1,630	2,256

Sources: Ministry of Finance; World Bank; and IMF staff estimates.

[1]Excluding extrabudgetary funds.

[2]Of which, 0.4 percent of GDP collected in noncash form.

[3]Of which, 1.8 percent of GDP collected in noncash form.

[4]Of which, 3.1 percent of GDP collected in noncash form.

[5]Excluding federal transfers.

1991 (which more than offset the registered improvement in the terms of trade for the Soviet Union) and, subsequently, disruptions to trade and financial relations among the former members of the U.S.S.R., which were especially pronounced in the early part of the transition period (1992–93), also contributed to the contraction of output in Russia. It is to the combination of these elements, adding up to a structurally induced drop in output, that the GDP losses must be mainly attributed (versus, say, the presence or absence at various times of a restrictive monetary policy) and that resulted in rising unemployment, a retrenchment of investment plans, cuts in production and a corresponding sharp erosion in the profitability of the enterprise sector, and the concomitant decline in revenue.[12] Barbone and Mar-

chetti (1995) argue that the decline in revenues seen in virtually all countries in the region must be seen in the context of the interconnection between expenditures on subsidies and profit taxes. They note that the net contribution of the enterprise sector to the budget, defined as profit taxes *net* of producer subsidies, has remained relatively stable and that the fiscal crisis is largely explained by a drop in turnover taxes and a relatively large increase in government expenditures (other than producer subsidies), mainly directed to the social sphere. In Russia, profit taxes, net of producer subsidies, amounted to about 4 percent of GDP in 1992; assuming that the bulk of producer subsidies had been phased out by 1994, net profit taxes had risen to some 7 percent of GDP by 1994. However, in Russia a large share of producer subsidies were off-budget.

Two other factors that may have influenced output are (1) the disorderly conditions that characterized

[12]Public investment fell from an estimated 11 percent of GDP in 1991 to 3 percent in 1992.

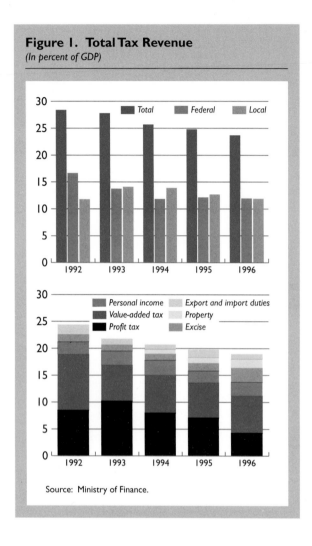

Figure 1. Total Tax Revenue
(In percent of GDP)

Source: Ministry of Finance.

base: enterprise profits. To the extent that the output contraction was also accompanied by increases in unemployment (and, hence, reductions in consumer demand), there has been a concomitant contraction of the base of other important taxes, such as taxes on wages and indirect taxes. In addition, tax rates have been reduced. The profit tax rate was reduced from 45 percent in 1991 to 35 percent in 1992; the VAT was reduced from 28 percent in 1992 to 20 percent in 1993; and other reductions also affected export duties and import tariff rates. In addition, the tax base has shrunk further, partly in response to legislative changes that—in the case of the profit tax—broadened the coverage of deductible expenditures, such as contributions to enterprise investment funds, and permitted higher depreciation allowances. Furthermore, the absence of an adequately hard budget constraint for the enterprise sector has led at times to payments arrears, especially during 1992–93, and a corresponding increase in tax arrears. At end-1995, tax arrears amounted to Rub 55 trillion (3½ percent of GDP); these had grown to Rub 125 trillion by end-1996 (equivalent to some 5½ percent of GDP), of which nearly Rub 70 trillion was due to the federal budget (Table 4 and Figure 4). The growth of tax arrears also reflects discretionary government action, particularly in the context of the introduction of the "30/70 rule."[13] Moreover, arrears in employer contributions to the Pension Fund have also grown and stood at over 2 percent of GDP by end-1996.

Far more important, the massive transfer of economic activity to the private sector has not only eroded the recorded tax bases but also greatly strained the administrative abilities of the tax authorities in a context of rapidly changing tax legislation. The complex institutional setup underlying the operations of a modern tax system, including modern accounting practices, computer facilities, and management expertise, simply did not exist when Russia embarked on reform. Russia's tax system was mainly set up to collect taxes from the publicly owned enterprise sector and was not equipped to deal with the proliferation of taxpayers that followed the introduction of new, broadly based taxes and the transfer of a growing share of value added to the emerging private sector. For instance, the number of organizations (commercial or otherwise) with a tax identification number and liable to remit individual

the transition, as managers and workers found themselves operating in uncharted territory where they learned through trial and error, with the associated inefficiencies; and (2) significant political instability and conflicting signals from the authorities as to the general direction of economic policy, involving, at times, sharp disagreements at senior policy levels that most likely undermined confidence in general. In addition, both *measured* output before the transition period and the initial output decline in the initial phase of the transition may have been overestimated (see Koen and Phillips, 1993).

While the output losses may explain a significant share of the real revenue decline, other forces have clearly been at work as well. The fall in the ratio of revenue to GDP has clearly reflected the different ways the transition has affected various sectors of the economy and, hence, the tax base. The much faster contraction of the industrial sector, for instance, has led to a relatively faster contraction of Russia's largest and traditionally most important tax

---

[13]The 30/70 rule allows enterprises to set aside 30 percent of their revenues for wage payments, even if in so doing they fail to fulfill all their tax obligations. The rule was introduced in the last quarter of 1994 for a fairly narrow set of enterprises fulfilling a number of strict conditions, but was considerably broadened in scope in early 1995, when the eligibility provisions were extended to all enterprises in the "productive" sector. The mechanism was phased out on March 1, 1996, but reintroduced again in August 1996.

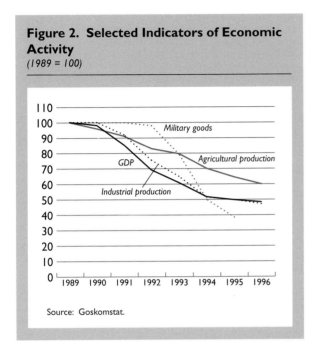

Figure 2. Selected Indicators of Economic Activity
(1989 = 100)

Source: Goskomstat.

Figure 3. Real Gross Industrial Output by Sector
(1990 = 100)

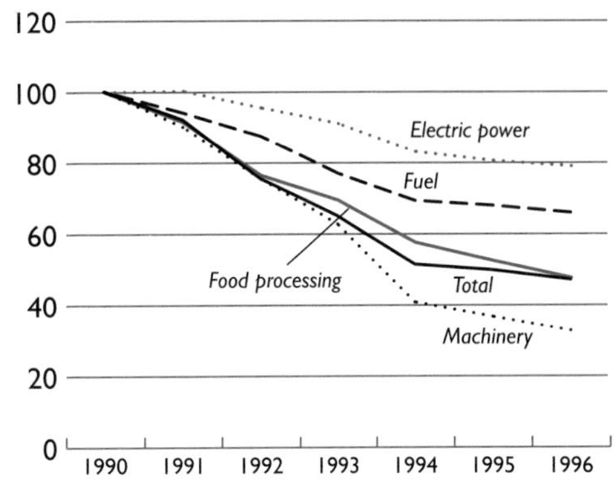

Source: Goskomstat.

income tax withheld at source or to pay some other tax stood, at end-1995, at 2.6 million. Of these, about 2.1 million were actually making profit tax payments, compared with 327,000 in 1990, a sixfold increase (Table 5). By the end of 1992, the year the VAT was introduced, 1.3 million enterprises were making payments; three years later, this number had risen to 2.1 million (Figure 5). At the same time, employment at the State Tax Service rose by 130 percent between end-1992 and end-1995.

Against the background of such heavy demands on the administrative capacities of the tax authorities, the government has not always acted in a consistent manner. A presidential decree issued in May 1994 that contained a number of tough (and simplifying) administrative measures designed to improve tax compliance was considerably undermined in early 1995 with the issuance of a counterdecree permitting enterprises once again to hold an unlimited number of settlement accounts with the banking system, thereby greatly complicating the ability of the tax authorities to monitor compliance. The new decree went so far as to point out the desirability of "improving the credit positions of enterprises and organizations" by way of justification.[14]

---

[14]See Decree of the President of the Russian Federation, No. 1006, May 23, 1994, "On Implementing a Complex of Measures to Achieve Timely and Complete Payment of Taxes and Other Obligatory Charges to the Budget," and Decree of the President of the Russian Federation, No. 291, March 21, 1995, "On Invalidating Clause 2 of Decree of the President of the Russian Federation No. 1006, dated May 23, 1994."

In addition to the emergence of new enterprises in the private sector, there has also been a massive transfer to the cash economy of previously recorded economic activity by established enterprises. Partly because of the high-inflation environment characteristic of the last several years, but mainly on account of the growing opportunities for tax evasion, enterprises now carry out a large proportion of their transactions on a cash basis, on the margins of the law. Indeed, a cottage industry has emerged in Russia specializing in facilitating and helping hide such transactions; making available, for a fee, large quantities of cash; and, in general, converting deposit rubles into cash rubles and/or foreign exchange. Only recently have the tax authorities begun to take small steps to come to grips with this situation. One aspect of this problem is the incentive that enterprises have had to shift transactions to the cash economy, given the role played by the banks. Under existing legislation, banks are free to dispose of balances in enterprise settlement accounts, for instance, to pay accrued tax obligations. Parallel to this process, the use of noncash forms of payment has increased; thus, not only have revenues declined but they have become less liquid, particularly at the local level, where up to one-third or more of revenue takes the form of in-kind payments, including fuel, utilities, and other commodities, in typically nontransparent arrangements between the enterprises and the local authorities. Furthermore, tax avoidance motivations have led to an upsurge of barter operations more generally.

Table 2. Selected Indicators of Economic Activity
(Real percent change over previous period)

	1990	1991	1992	1993	1994	1995	1996
Gross domestic product	–3	–5	–15	–9	–13	–4	–6
Industrial production	...	–8	–18	–14	–21	–3	–5
Extraction industries	–3	–4	–11	–10	–10	–2	...
Processing industries	...	–8	–19	–15	–24	–5	...
Of which:							
Consumer goods	7	–1	–15	–11	–21	–12	–7
Military goods	...	...	–21	–19	–37	–23	–24
Agricultural production	–4	–5	–9	–4	–12	–8	–7
Crops	–8	0	–5	–3	–10	–5	–9
Livestock	–1	–7	–12	–5	–13	–13	–8
Freight (railroad)	–3	–9	–16	–18	–21	–3	–8

Source: Goskomstat.

In addition, there has at times been a visible tendency to apply tax legislation in a discretionary manner, with key sectors, enterprises, and regions enjoying significant exemptions during much of the transition period, as a form of implicit subsidization.

Indeed, one of the key characteristics of the Russian tax system before 1992 was the existence of relatively high tax rates, which coexisted with generous tax exemptions and preferences to specific sectors, industries, and/or regions. Recourse to exemptions

Table 3. Real Gross Industrial Output by Sector[1]
(Real percent change over previous period)

	1991	1992	1993	1994	1995	1996	1991–96 Cumulative
Electric power generation	0	–5	–5	–9	–3	–2	–21
Fuel	–6	–7	–12	–10	–1	–3	–34
Ferrous metallurgy	–7	–16	–17	–17	10	–4	–44
Nonferrous metallurgy	–9	–25	–14	–9	3	–5	–48
Chemicals[2]	–8	–23	–20	–20	7	–11	–56
Petrochemicals[3]	–3	–19	–25	–35	10	...	–58
Machinery	–10	–16	–17	–33	–9	–11	–66
Forestry, timber processing, and pulp and paper	–9	–15	–19	–30	–1	–22	–62
Construction materials	–2	–20	–16	–27	–8	–25	–67
Light industry	–9	–30	–23	–46	–30	–28	–87
Food processing	–10	–16	–9	–17	–8	–9	–52
Total	–8	–18	–14	–21	–3	–5	–53

Source: Goskomstat.
[1]Data for medium and large enterprises.
[2]Starting from 1996, chemical and petrochemical industries are combined.
[3]Cumulative decline for petrochemicals excludes 1996.

Table 4. Tax Arrears
(In trillions of rubles)

	Total	VAT	Profit	Excise	Personal Income and Property	Other
Tax arrears on January 1, 1996	55.0	25.5	16.6	3.0	5.2	4.7
Federal	30.0	18.5	6.6	2.8	—	2.1
Regional	25.0	7.0	10.0	0.2	5.2	2.6
Tax arrears on May 1, 1996	102.2	42.0	24.4	10.7	7.0	18.1
Federal	56.2	30.9	9.9	8.2	—	7.2
Regional	46.0	11.1	14.5	2.5	7.0	10.9
Tax arrears on January 1, 1997	125.1	55.8	20.7	12.5	13.6	22.5
Federal	68.2	42.1	9.2	10.1	—	6.8
Regional	56.9	13.7	11.5	2.4	13.6	15.7
Memorandum items:		July 1, 1997				
Tax arrears		164.1				
Federal		84.1				
Regional		79.7				
Arrears to extrabudgetary funds		124.1				
Wage arrears[1]		55.3				

Sources: State Tax Service; and Goskomstat.
[1]Excluding in the military.

made the tax system more distortionary and resulted in large amounts of forgone revenue,[15] which in turn undermined the government's ability to respond more effectively to growing needs, particularly human capital investment and infrastructure. Understandably, the uneven distribution of the tax burden, in turn, helped maintain an environment in which tax evasion was rampant, pressures for new and/or broader exemptions were ever present, and the tax base was under constant threat of further erosion.[16]

The government introduced at times contingency measures during the transition period to offset the larger than expected revenue drop. For instance, in the context of the authorities' 1994 economic program, the government sought to eliminate VAT exemptions, improve the collection of existing excises on natural gas, repeal import duty exemptions, introduce a withholding tax on personal interest income and a per ton tax on oil assessed in dollars, and in-

crease the gasoline tax. While the revenue impact of these (and other) measures was expected to amount to 4 percent of GDP, in the event additional revenues amounted to about 1 percent of GDP. By and large, the effect of the government's efforts was limited, with delays in implementation (often reflecting the absence of political consensus on the desirability of the measures) significantly lowering projected rev-

---

[15]A case in point is the tax exemptions granted to the National Sports Foundation in 1993 that were intended to support athletes' preparation for the Atlanta Olympic Games, and that in the end were used to allow the importation of a broad array of commodities free of customs duties, VAT, and excises. In time, this organization became the main importer of tobacco, distilled spirits, and cars in Russia, with a yearly turnover variously estimated to have reached $3–4 billion.

[16]For a listing of some of the tax exemptions in force during 1992–96, see the Appendix.

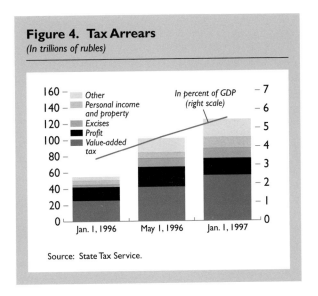

Figure 4. Tax Arrears
(In trillions of rubles)

Source: State Tax Service.

Table 5. Number of Taxpayers
(In thousands, end of period)

	1990	1991	1992	1993	1994	1995
Registered taxpayers[1]	—	—	—	—	2,478.0	2,553.0
Profit tax[2]	327.3	647.8	1,326.0	1,840.8	2,080.1	2,132.2
VAT[2]	—	—	1,330.1	1,853.9	2,112.2	2,173.0
Personal income tax	561.2	837.9	1,473.3	1,995.5	2,258.5	2,336.8
Excise tax	—	—	17.0	5.0	5.9	6.4

Source: State Tax Service.

[1]Organizations (commercial or otherwise) with a tax identification number and liable to remit individual income tax withheld at source or to pay some other tax.

[2]Actually making payments.

enues. This was particularly the case for a number of measures (for example, including interest in the definition of taxable income) that, while supported by the government, did not receive the support in parliament necessary to change the underlying legislation.

Role of Tax Reform

Before the onset of economic reforms in late 1991 and early 1992, Russia's tax system (consisting, essentially, of the residual transfer of profits to the state, after deductions for various enterprise funds)

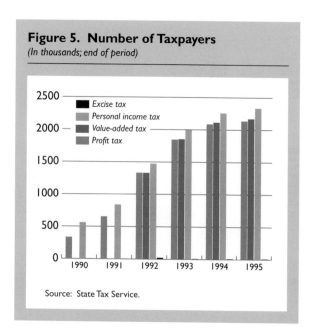

Figure 5. Number of Taxpayers
(In thousands; end of period)

Source: State Tax Service.

was not compatible with the efficient functioning of a market economy. Because economic agents did not function as reasonably autonomous decision-making entities, taxes did not have the effects on individual economic behavior generally observed in market economies (for example, payroll taxes and the effects on individual labor supply behavior). So many features distinguished a given Soviet tax from its market-economy counterpart that it may actually be somewhat misleading to think of them as being the same tax. One example was the enterprise profit tax (it accounted for nearly one-third of total budgetary revenues in the Soviet Union by 1990), which expropriated rather than taxed the profits of state-owned enterprises and arbitrarily defined allowable expenses, exemptions, and deductions (for example, to various funds for social development, and for research and development). Moreover, the tax often differed by branch of industry or by enterprise to even out profitability and, in the context of the soft budget constraints characteristic of that era, was frequently waived altogether for enterprises that demonstrated financial need. Because the state played the role of both taxpayer and tax collector, profit taxes were often subject to a great deal of bargaining at the enterprise level and were usually fully determined only ex post.

A number of considerations can be identified in Russia as having driven the authorities in the direction of tax reform. Key among them were the need to eliminate the most glaring distortions and to restructure the tax system in a way that enhanced the transparency and efficiency of existing taxes and that brought the system closer to internationally accepted norms; the need to provide an adequate level of revenue to support Russia's macroeconomic stabilization efforts as other traditional sources of revenue dried up (for example, profit taxes, following the large-scale transfer of enterprises to the private sector and the associated difficulties in monitoring their activities); and the need to have tax reform support other aspects of economic reform (for example, the system of incentives and signals in the economy at large). These reforms have included the introduction of value-added and excise taxes (1992); the movement away from the multiplicity of turnover taxes levied at a broad range of product-specific rates; the introduction of schedular personal income taxes; the adoption of a profit tax to replace confiscatory profit taking from the enterprise sector; and the conversion of nontariff trade barriers to ad valorem duties. In addition, privatization receipts have emerged as another source of revenue.

At present, Russia's tax system suffers from a number of deficiencies that have contributed to the emergence of a somewhat incongruous situation: rapidly declining revenues and simultaneous complaints from taxpayers about high tax burdens and arbitrary administration of existing tax legislation. The basic legal tax provisions remain embodied in a large collection of legislative acts and presidential decrees that have been put together with no attempt at consistency or administrative simplicity. Some of this reflects Russia's special circumstances during the early part of the transition period: radical transformations in the structure of the economy and the perceived interests of various social groups, and changes in the political environment, which often revealed the lack of consensus on the aims and means of economic reform and which frequently resulted in the emergence of sectoral pressures for tax relief and privileges. Thus, rather than being based on a few clear, coherent, and easy-to-understand tax laws, Russia's existing tax legislation is based on a number of laws, resolutions, and decrees, each reflecting a balance of prevailing interests and compromises. In addition, tax laws have been subject to unpredictable and frequent changes; both the VAT and the profit tax law, for instance, were amended 12 times each during 1992–95.[17] These changes have resulted in the emergence of a number of undesirable features in particular taxes; some of the most important are identified below.

Value-Added Tax

Two VAT rates (10 percent and 28 percent) emerged in 1992 with nontransparent rules as to what was taxable at what rate; a large number of ex-

emptions also created the usual complexities for taxpayers engaged in both taxable and exempt activities. (For instance, food products are assessed a lower—10 percent—rate, but the definition of food has sometimes been interpreted broadly and, until 1995, included all raw materials used in the agricultural sector.) The experiences of many other countries have shown that maintaining a VAT with several rates and generous exemptions leads to high administrative and compliance costs and encourages tax evasion. If the intention of the authorities was to offset the regressive impact of the VAT on low-income groups, a better mechanism would have been targeted transfer payments through some income-support system, which they could have financed from the resources they generated by taxing foodstuffs at the standard rate and limiting exemptions to a few items, such as bread and milk.

Some of the original deficiencies in the definition of the VAT base have gradually been corrected. For instance, imports were included in the base in early 1993; food imports, which had been exempted, began to be taxed in mid-1995. Deductions for the VAT invoiced on purchases of capital equipment, which were not allowed initially, began to be permitted. The deductions could be spread in equal installments over a 24-month period as of 1993, and the period was further reduced to six months beginning in mid-1995. As of April 1, 1996, such tax credits were allowed on a full and immediate basis, thus eliminating an important distortion that, for a time, had discouraged productive investment, although it also induced some short-term adverse effects on revenues. More important, in July 1995 the practice whereby an enterprise could claim VAT credits at the time of production rather than at the time of payment was formally abandoned.

A number of other problems, however, remain. Chief among these one can point to the following:

- The invoice credit method for VAT determination has not been extended to the retail and service sectors, which means that, since the introduction of the VAT, Russia has been operating under a dual system of rules, one for manufacturers and one for distributors.[18] This creates serious complications for control, because it requires that a clear distinction be drawn between a taxpayer that is a manufacturer (wholesaler) and one that is a retailer[19] and it imposes com-

---

[17]For instance, new versions of the VAT law were issued on May 22, July 16, and December 22, 1992; February 25 and March 6, 1993; November 11 and December 6, 1994; and April 25, June 23, August 7, August 22, and November 30, 1995.

[18]Manufacturers' liability is determined as the difference between the VAT charged on sales and the VAT paid on purchases, whereas wholesalers, retailers, and caterers are taxed on gross margins, or the difference between selling and buying prices.

[19]This distinction is sometimes difficult to make; for instance, is an enterprise engaged in assembling or repairing part of the manufacturing or the retail sector?

pliance costs on retailers—which can be high in periods of high inflation—associated with the holding of inventories and the need to reestimate the markup on a monthly basis. Moreover, because this dual system of rules facilitates evasion, it has a negative impact on revenues.

- A hybrid system exists for VAT on foreign trade, namely, on an origin basis for trade within the Commonwealth of Independent States (CIS) and on a destination basis for trade outside the CIS, creating problems for transshipment and trade rerouting, especially through customs union countries (for example, Belarus).
- There is an occasional separate surcharge (3 percent in 1994, 1.5 percent in 1995) that uses the same base as the VAT and for which an independent return must be filed and a separate payment order prepared, thereby considerably increasing the administrative burden on the tax authorities and the enterprise sector.[20]
- At present, there is no requirement for mandatory issuing of VAT invoices, which severely undermines tax auditing.
- The discretionary use of exemptions continues; the VAT on imports at the full rate is estimated to have been paid on only some 30–40 percent of recorded imports during 1995–96.

These as well as other features have severely undermined the simplicity of the VAT and contributed to a shrinking of the tax base that might otherwise have been avoided.

Profit Tax

Perhaps the key issue affecting the yield of the profit tax during the transition period is low effective tax rates resulting from the existence of various special allowances and concessions. Together with losses carried forward from earlier years, total deductions can reach up to 50 percent of pretax profits. Allowable deductions (in addition to depreciation) are identified in Article 6 of the profit tax law (the longest article in the law) and exist for "capital investments intended for the purpose of production, for housing construction and also for paying off bank credits obtained and used for these purposes, including the interest on such credits" (section 1a of the article); "enterprises' expenditures on the maintenance of health, educational, cultural and sports facilities and institutions, child care centers, summer camps" (section 1b); enterprise outlays for "con-

ducting scientific research and research and development activities" (section 1g); plus a number of other sector-specific allowances for a broad range of activities. In addition, section 4 of the same article contains special provisions for the exemption of the profit tax during a four-year period (the first two years at 100 percent, declining to 50 percent in the third year and 25 percent in the fourth year) for newly created "small enterprises engaged in the production and processing of agricultural products, in the manufacture of consumer goods, construction materials, medical equipment, medicines, housing construction, housing repair," among others.

The sections of the profit tax law that regulate the implementation of these concessions is general enough to permit any enterprise to carry out the bulk of its investment program under one of the above provisions. At a time when much of the country's industrial base is undergoing modernization and/or conversion, most enterprises have found it quite easy in practice to view the creation of new assets as contributing to these processes and, therefore, as being eligible for the relevant deductions. Thus, during much of 1992–96, the taxable base was reduced by such investments, significantly cutting into the revenues generated by the most important Russian tax. Beyond the revenue impact, it is clear that the existence of such concessions requires higher tax rates for a given level of profits and creates enormous complications in tax administration. Given the general language used in the legislation, a potential area of conflict between the tax authorities and the enterprise sector immediately emerges, creating a ripe environment for corruption, arbitrariness, and resource misallocation.

Until January 1, 1996, when it was finally eliminated, the profit tax base included wages paid in excess of the equivalent of six times the minimum wage.[21] This provision of the profit tax legislation had been seen as a mechanism for moderating wage increases and for preserving a certain level of profit transfers to the budget that might otherwise have simply been distributed in the form of higher wages. The excess wage provision was extended to privately owned enterprises but exempted foreign-owned businesses. While in practice nearly 25 percent of the total profit tax collected originated with the tax on excess wages, the tax itself is thought to have introduced a number of distortions and inefficiencies. It may have discouraged the growth of the entrepreneurial sector in domestic enterprises at a time when such managerial capacities were very much in need of being developed. Because the tax on excess wages did not become effective until total enterprise profits

---

[20]Although the surcharge was eliminated in 1996, the possibility of its reintroduction reemerges every year as discussions on the budget get under way in parliament and last-minute efforts are made to find additional revenues.

[21]During 1992–93, the threshold was set at the equivalent of four minimum wages.

were positive, it did not affect excess wage payments in profitable and unprofitable enterprises equally. As in other cases with such nontransparent mechanisms, additional problems for tax administration were created. These problems were associated with the interpretation of the regulatory provisions and the opportunities for abuse.

The Tax System

Five main taxes (VAT, corporate profits, personal income, excises, and customs duties) account for the bulk of total tax revenue. In practice, however, a presidential decree issued in December 1993 clarifying various aspects of the relationship between the federal budget and the budgets of the members of the federation allows the regional and local authorities to introduce new taxes not envisaged in the tax legislation.[22] Understandably, this decree led to a proliferation of new taxes and to a pervasive sense in broad segments of the enterprise sector that if all taxes due were actually paid, most economic activity would be rendered unprofitable.[23] In the absence of appropriate coordination between the tax demands of the center and those of the regions, it is perhaps not surprising that tax evasion has become pervasive, tax arrears have grown, the government itself has had to take initiatives to allow enterprises to defer payment of various taxes (and, subsequently, to agree to their rescheduling), and, in the process, tax enforcement and administration have become arbitrary and unpredictable.

A climate characterized by the absence of legality and due acceptance of and respect for the law has emerged. This element of unpredictability in the tax system—linked to the large and highly variable number of taxes and the nominal levels of taxation that they imply in the aggregate—has introduced considerable uncertainty in the investment climate. It is increasingly difficult to know whether activities that are profitable today will remain so tomorrow, given the operation of the tax system; this uncertainty in turn has discouraged the long-range planning and investment that are essential for the recovery and modernization of the Russian economy.

There is thus an overwhelming need to simplify the tax system, to eliminate a number of taxes with small yields, and to carefully circumscribe the jurisdiction of local and regional authorities in the area of tax legislation. The disorderly conditions have also undermined the credibility of the system underlying intergovernmental fiscal relations—there is evidence of a growing number of regions entering into "special" fiscal regimes with the federal government, involving, among other things, the remittance to the federal budget of a smaller VAT share from the region than called for in the law, or "single-channel" agreements whereby established revenue-sharing formulas are bypassed altogether and the regional government makes a single payment to the federal budget.

The authorities took an important step to address some of these deficiencies in the first half of 1997, presenting to the Duma a draft tax code whose chief purposes are to (1) bring into a single document all the disparate pieces of "legislation" presently regulating Russia's tax environment while establishing a common terminology and laying out clearly defined procedures for the payment of taxes; (2) reduce the number of taxes collected at all levels of government from some 75–80 at present (as far as is known) to no more than 25–30; and (3) define the rights and obligations of taxpayers and the tax authorities and the avenues of legal redress available to both. While the draft tax code was approved on first reading, eventual promulgation is unlikely before mid-1998.

Another feature of Russia's tax system is its revenue structure, which differs from that prevailing in other countries, say, those belonging to the OECD. As shown in Table 6, while the share of personal income taxes, corporate profit taxes, and taxes on goods and services in total tax revenues in the OECD account, on average, for some 37 percent, 11 percent, and 43 percent, respectively, the corresponding shares in Russia are closer to 10 percent, 29 percent, and 40 percent, respectively. The reasons for this distribution stem from the state's traditional role in the Russian economy of main intermediary and distributor of resources through the budget. Given the large share of public services that were financed through the budget, wage levels were necessarily understated. With wages being "monetized" and with wage determination increasingly becoming a market-determined process, however, there has been a sharp increase in the level of wages and a distinct rise in their variance across the labor market. At the same time, it remains a medium-term priority of the government to gradually reduce the many hidden subsidies provided to employers in the public sector, with wages being adjusted upward. By establishing a closer link between productivity and benefit levels, wage policy should encourage the development of

---

[22]Decree of the President of the Russian Federation No. 2268 of December 22, 1993 states that "in the republics within the Russian Federation, its territories, regions and autonomous formations, and the cities of Moscow and St. Petersburg, additional taxes and dues not provided for by the legislation of the Russian Federation may be introduced by decisions of the organs of state power of the subjects of the Russian Federation and of the local organs of state power."

[23]A draft law approved by the Duma (parliament) in late 1995 "On the Fundamentals of the Tax System of the Russian Federation" actually identified no fewer than 75–80 known taxes and fees in existence at the federal, regional, and local levels.

Table 6. Selected Countries: General Government Tax Revenue, 1995[1]
(In percent of GDP)

	Taxes on Income, Profits, and Capital Gains	Of which: Profits	Taxes on Goods and Services	Total Tax Revenue
Industrial countries				
Australia	17.1	4.6	9.0	30.9
Canada	17.1	3.0	9.5	31.0
Denmark	31.0	2.1	16.6	49.7
Germany	11.8	1.1	10.9	23.8
Italy	14.5	3.6	11.3	28.2
Sweden	20.6	3.1	12.1	35.2
United Kingdom	13.0	3.3	12.3	29.0
United States	12.8	2.6	5.0	20.9
European Union countries[2]	14.4	2.9	12.8	29.6
OECD—Europe[2]	13.3	2.8	13.0	28.6
OECD—Total[2]	13.3	3.0	11.9	27.6

Source: Organization for Economic Cooperation and Development, *Revenue Statistics,* 1997.
[1]Excluding social security.
[2]Unweighted average.

the private sector and contribute to the creation of a broader base for the income tax. Furthermore, the recent elimination of the allowable wage deduction for the calculation of enterprises' taxable profits (equivalent to six minimum wages) should also contribute to a redistribution of taxes away from profits and in favor of the personal income tax.

An additional feature of Russia's tax system is the energy sector's relatively low contribution to tax revenues. While the oil and gas sectors in 1995 accounted for some 18 percent of GDP, their combined contribution to the budget amounted to about 3½–4 percent of GDP. The relative tax burden for this sector in 1995, defined as the ratio of oil and gas revenues to total revenues, divided by the share of the sector in GDP, was one-third to one-half that in most other energy-producing countries.[24]

Exemptions

By far the most challenging issue in the area of tax reform in the period ahead is tax exemptions. Tax revenues during the transition have been severely undermined by the general and specific exemptions

granted at various times to various sectors and enterprises, across a broad range of taxes. While frequently motivated by the perceived need to support key sectors of the economy or, more generally, boost economic activity, these exemptions have often reflected the lobbying efforts of key constituencies representing various vested interests. Furthermore, these exemptions have often been taken by various agencies within the government on their initiative, with no attempt to examine the macroeconomic or budgetary impact of the exemptions. Indeed, no attempt has been made thus far to identify the budgetary cost of these exemptions, for instance, in the preparation of the draft budget, partly because no single agency has a comprehensive listing of all exemptions in place. A situation emerged, therefore, where there was virtually no tax for which there was not some form of exemption and there was no sector that did not enjoy or seek some form of tax relief. In time, this state of affairs led to the emergence of a culture where tax privileges were the rule rather than the exception and, given the inequities that were inevitably created, pressures for new and broader exemptions multiplied.

While the direct revenue impact of many of these exemptions was often not large, some did have an appreciably heavy effect on the budget. Among these, one can single out exemptions to the payment of oil export duties that, during 1994, became nearly uni-

[24]Gray (forthcoming) estimates that for the oil and gas sector in Russia, actual revenues were about 54 percent of notional liability, defined as tax revenues assuming full compliance with the law and without exemptions.

versal and exemptions given to the National Sports Foundation and other organizations deemed charitable (for example, Afghan War Veterans' Union), which applied to import duties, excises, and the VAT. In the context of an otherwise tight budgetary situation, these exemptions made fiscal adjustment more difficult than was necessary and, by reinforcing a growing culture of nonpayment, may have contributed to the large growth of tax arrears seen during and after 1995. Monitoring and supervising these exemptions also placed heavy demands on the administrative abilities of the authorities and led to perceptions of unfairness in the tax system, which have not contributed to creating a culture of tax compliance.[25]

Tax Administration

In Russia, as in other countries in transition, tax administration has evolved in a way that does not put enough emphasis on voluntary compliance, that is, the responsibility of taxpayers to determine their own tax liabilities as well as to report and pay their taxes on time. No doubt because the tax administration system until recently was largely geared to collecting taxes mainly from the enterprise sector, large-scale involvement by tax officials is seen as a necessary ingredient of effective tax administration. This approach contrasts with the principles of self-assessment and voluntary compliance on which modern tax systems in market economies are based. Because of the large increase in the number of taxpayers in recent years (reflecting, for instance, the emerging private sector and such developments as the introduction of broadly based consumption taxes such as the VAT), the bulk of the tax administration resources are being allocated to routine functions associated with tax reporting by taxpayers, with little attention being given to audit and control.

A key priority for tax administration in Russia therefore is to move to a system based on the principles that prevail in market economies, which will allow officials to focus their attention on those taxpayers who fail to comply with existing tax legislation and regulations. As part of this, it will be necessary to introduce more specialization in the functions of the staff at the State Tax Service so as to support a system based on self-assessment (for example, processing returns, collecting tax arrears, and carrying out audits). Efficiency gains obtained through specialization would free State Tax Service staff who could be released from routine undertakings and redirected to enforcement activities. The need for such gains is underscored by the significant deficiencies

that exist in other areas. Among these may be cited: (1) an inadequate level of coordination between the center and the regions in terms of the work of various organizations performing a number of tax administration and collection functions such as customs offices, branches of the central bank, and currency control bodies;[26] (2) the need to monitor more closely the evolution of tax exemptions (which in Russia emanate from a broad range of different sources, including the office of the President, the Prime Minister, the Ministry of Finance, and various government dependencies); (3) the absence of an effective system of computerization that will provide a master file of registered taxpayers, which would facilitate the identification of delinquent taxpayers and allow tax inspectors to distinguish appropriate cases for audit and control; (4) the unavailability of detailed statistical information on the size and the structure of the tax base and the tax burden for certain categories of taxpayers, including detailed sectoral identification of each, which would allow analysis of the implications of changes proposed to existing tax legislation; (5) the need to create a streamlined accounting framework, with forms and procedures considerably simplified so as not to discourage taxpayers from completing them and fulfilling their tax obligations in a timely manner; and (6) the need for greater attention on the collection of tax arrears, which have grown rapidly in recent years.

Furthermore, it is necessary to complement reforms in the above areas with a credible system of penalties that are both severe enough and credible enough to discourage noncompliance. Taxpayers must believe, from experience, that if they fail to comply with tax regulations or, in general, if they understate their tax liabilities, there is a high risk that they will be caught and that the associated interest charges and penalties will more than offset any potential benefit of evasion. These conditions are not in place in Russia as yet; during the first half of 1995, criminal legal proceedings for tax evasion were initiated against 1,658 individuals and enterprises. Only 216 were ultimately submitted to the courts, resulting in 107 convictions. At the same time, penalties should be imposed within the margins of the law and be balanced by an appeals process designed to protect taxpayers' rights.

It may also be desirable to introduce incentives for taxpayers to act within the framework of the law. The more they come to see the advantages of compliance (other than the fear of penalties), the more successful tax collection is likely to be. Many have

---

[25]The draft tax code presently under consideration envisages a substantial reduction in the number of exemptions.

[26]Less than 1 percent of the entire staff of the State Tax Service (about 160,000 employees) works at headquarters; this number may have to be significantly increased if some of the coordinating functions are to be enhanced.

pointed out the potential benefits of education campaigns designed to highlight, for instance, the utility of VAT receipts as essential components of consumer protection, legal redress, and so on. In countries with high social security contribution rates, powerful incentives for evasion exist, leading sometimes to informal arrangements between employers and employees. But if the majority of benefits are linked to these contributions (as opposed to being available across the board), then employees will have strong incentives to register. Finally, the state must win the confidence of the population that it will use these resources well and that its policies will be guided by the desire to protect the interests of the population rather than to preserve the benefits and privileges of lobby groups. As noted by Etzioni (1988), "studies have found a relatively close association between the sense that taxes are fairly imposed, the sense of the legitimacy of the government and the purposes for which revenues are used, and the extent of tax evasion."

Penalties and Fines

One area in which reforms are needed is the system of penalties and fines. The present system of fines is not based on sound principles, is at times unduly harsh (and for that reason ineffective), and contains elements of arbitrariness, which must be corrected. Some examples will illustrate this general principle.

(1) When an enterprise wrongly includes some item as a cost of production in calculating profit tax liabilities, the penalty is equal to eight times the amount included. The corresponding penalty in the case of the VAT is the amount of the cost included. The reasons for the sharply differential treatment are not clear. It is thus necessary to move to a system that links penalties not to the tax base but to the amounts not actually paid to the budget. There are in place numerous other penalties associated with, for example, inaccurate keeping of accounting books, inhospitable treatment of tax inspectors, and so on, which have made the system at times vulnerable to abuse and corruption.

(2) The authorities also need to address a provision in the existing tax legislation that deals with cases of enterprises that conclude sales contracts at fictitious prices so as to reduce their profit tax liabilities. As presently enforced, this provision states that the tax authorities have the right to value the goods at market prices in such cases where there is a presumption of underreporting. Enterprises have argued that in Russia's present financial situation, characterized by a large outstanding stock of interenterprise arrears, they are often forced to sell at cut-rate prices. Then they are visited by a tax inspector who

arbitrarily passes judgment on the market price and punishes the enterprise for alleged underreporting. There would thus appear to be a need to make antievasion regulations more transparent.

(3) Under established practice, enterprises make three advance payments of the profit tax during the quarter on the basis of estimated profits. Because they are allowed to make their own estimates, they have, in the past, tended to underestimate expected profits. In the highly inflationary environment characteristic of the early part of the transition, underestimating profits was tantamount to receiving a zero-interest loan from the budget. In late 1993, this anomaly was corrected, and enterprises that underestimated profits were required to pay interest on the difference between the actual tax due and the total amount paid in advance, with the rate assessed at the central bank refinance rate. In those cases where the enterprise was due a refund, the Ministry of Finance would also pay the refinance rate on the overpayment. Subsequently proposals were put forward to make the system asymmetric; that is, the enterprise would continue to be punished when actual profits exceeded estimated profits, but the ministry would refund the difference without interest when the reverse was true. Predictably, this led to complaints of arbitrariness and unfairness in the implementation of penalty provisions.

The ultimate objective should be to have a system of penalties that is simple, predictable, and consistent with the constitution and other tax legislation. Taxpayers often make the case that most violations are due not to deliberate tax evasion but rather to the inability of enterprises to keep up with the morass of rapidly changing and difficult-to-interpret tax regulations.

Appendix. Major Tax Exemptions in Force, 1992–96

This appendix lists some of the most important formal tax exemptions in force in Russia during 1992–96. No attempt is made at comprehensiveness; rather, the aim is to identify those exemptions with the largest impact in terms of forgone revenue or those that are more likely to be abused.

Profit Tax

(1) Enterprises' contributions to "special extrabudgetary funds," from which they are able to finance certain capital intensive projects (for example, plant modernization and reconstruction of pipelines in the oil sector), are included as a cost of production and deducted from taxable profits. The rates (as a percentage of the cost of production) vary from sector to sector but can be as high as 3 percent. Decree

No. 1004 of May 23, 1994 (section 4) called for the elimination of these funds as of July 1 of that year and suggested that they be consolidated into the federal budget. But the decree was largely ignored on this point and these funds existed throughout 1995, further eroding the profit tax base. The funds were phased out in early 1996.

(2) All enterprise expenditures for capital investments "intended for the purpose of production" as well as investment in construction, including housing construction, are exempt from the taxable base. Repayment of bank credits obtained in connection with the above activities is also deductible. This latter exemption also includes purchases of transportation equipment used in construction and certain types of machinery.

(3) Expenditures by enterprises that provide social services to workers, including those for the maintenance of health, educational, cultural, and other facilities, are exempt from the profit tax.

(4) Newly created small enterprises engaged in the production and processing of agricultural products and in the manufacture of consumer goods, construction materials, medical equipment, medicines, housing construction, and housing repair are exempt from paying the profit tax for two years following registration. The tax is set at 25 percent and 50 percent of the prevailing rate during the third and fourth year, respectively. Enterprises are expected to repay the taxes only if they cease operations after the end of the fifth year following registration.

(5) Enterprises' contributions to charitable organizations, typically up to 3 percent of the taxable base, are exempt from the profit tax.

The cumulative deductions listed above (in items 1–5) may not exceed more than 50 percent of the taxable base.

(6) Enterprises' contributions to reserve funds, up to 15 percent of the taxable base (10 percent in 1995), are also exempt.

(7) Voluntary donations to campaign funds for the election of officials to federal, regional, or local bodies may be deducted from the tax base, up to the equivalent of 10,000 minimum wages in the case of federal bodies.

(8) Other exemptions are granted to certain specialized enterprises (for example, television and radio broadcasting companies and consumer cooperatives situated in the territories of the far north) and to religious and invalids' organizations.

(9) Since 1994, the republic of Ingushetia has enjoyed special "offshore" tax status within the Russian Federation. Any enterprise registered in Ingushetia is exempt from paying regional or local taxes (profit taxes, property taxes, and certain social taxes) and is refunded, through funds provided by the federal government to the republic, the federal share of the profit tax and 50 percent of the VAT. The original idea was to provide incentives to enterprises to move operations to the poorest oblast in the Federation; in practice, however, because the profit tax law is ambiguous on the issue of registration and location of the physical plant, many enterprises have reregistered in Ingushetia and have thus benefited from the tax exemption, but have not actually moved operations to the republic.

(10) The 30/70 rule allows enterprises to set aside 30 percent of their revenues for wage payments, even if in so doing they fail to fulfill all their tax obligations. The rule was introduced in the last quarter of 1994 for a fairly narrow set of enterprises that met a number of strict conditions, but was considerably broadened in scope in early 1995, when the eligibility provisions were extended to all enterprises in the productive sphere. The mechanism was phased out on March 1, 1996, but reintroduced again in August 1996.

Value-Added Tax

(1) A comprehensive VAT exemption on housing construction (building materials and labor services) was introduced on January 1, 1993 and remained in force until May 1, 1995. While in force, the exemption applied to all forms of construction by the enterprise sector, including for residential and/or social purposes, and also affected repairs, maintenance, and renovations.

(2) State Customs Committee Directive No. 248 of April 13, 1995 exempted all entities importing technological equipment from paying the VAT and the special (VAT) tax. According to the directive, any merchandise "used to manufacture goods or means of production shall be regarded as technological equipment." The list of equipment, given in an attachment, was eight pages long. Goods not specified in that attachment may also, in any event, be exempted at the discretion of the State Customs Committee. Certain types of transport equipment are also exempted, including cruise boats and "other analogous" ships, civilian helicopters, and other civilian aircraft. The exemption was made retroactive to December 10, 1994. All taxes already collected between that date and April 13, 1995 were to be refunded to the importers. Attempts were made in late 1995 to revoke this exemption, but these failed.

(3) Until mid-1995, imported food was exempt from the VAT. In addition, all food products and certain children's items were assessed at the lower rate of 10 percent, but the definition of food products was applied liberally and included, for instance, virtually all raw materials used in the agricultural sector. Proposals were put forward in late 1994 to dras-

tically reduce the list of food items that were assessed at the lower rate (basically, it was proposed to include only those items that were part of the minimum consumption basket at that time) and to include all imported food at the same rate as the one corresponding to the domestically produced item. After some delay, this measure was approved in mid-1995, with the list of products assessed at the lower rate consisting of 16 products deemed to be essential.

(4) In late 1995, and effective January 1, 1996, enterprises in the mass media received a full exemption on the payment of VAT (as well as on the payment of import duties) on purchases of an extensive list of goods needed for the production process.

(5) All "scientific research and experimental and design work financed from the state budget," as well as independent research paid for by educational institutions—encompassing such areas as agriculture, mining, and research in various fields, including purchases of equipment and services required to carry out such scientific work—are also exempt from the VAT.

(6) City transit services and commuter passenger services by sea, river, rail, and road are exempt from the VAT.

(7) Housing rents are exempt from the VAT.

(8) Goods and services manufactured by enterprises in which at least 50 percent of the workforce is disabled are exempt from the VAT.

(9) New VAT exemptions were introduced in 1995 for the economic activities of prisons, labor camps (for instance, those attached to the timber and mining industry), and other security-related institutions.

Excises

(1) The list of excisable goods was reduced in late 1994 with the exclusion of automobile tires, trucks, fine wines, furs, genuine leather clothes, yachts, motor boats, hunting guns, and carpets, among other items. The list was reduced further in 1995 and, as of end-1996, included only alcoholic beverages, cigarettes, gasoline, precious metals, and oil and gas.

(2) Beginning in mid-1993, the National Sports Foundation was exempted from paying excise duties on all its imports. By the time this exemption was withdrawn, on October 1, 1995 for alcohol, and on December 1, 1995 for tobacco, the National Sports Foundation had become Russia's largest importer of vodka, other spirits, and cigarettes, with an annual turnover estimated to amount to $3–4 billion.

(3) Excise tax exemptions on sales of domestically produced cars were also granted to various enterprises selectively throughout the period under review, often in the form of temporary reductions in rates.

Customs Duties

(1) Exemptions on the payment of duties on oil exports began to be granted in early 1994 and were made nearly universal by the end of the year, but were eliminated in the 1995 budget.

(2) Beginning in mid-1993, the National Sports Foundation was exempted from paying customs duties on its imports. This exemption was terminated on October 1, 1995 for alcohol and on December 1 for tobacco, although the foundation received compensation from the budget (amounting to some $200 million) through the end of the year. Through satellite organizations affiliated to the foundation, virtually all cars and alcohol and tobacco products imported in the two years to mid-1995 were exempted from the payment of import duties. The revenue impact of the elimination of these exemptions, however, was minimal because a similar exemption was granted in Belarus shortly thereafter. Since Belarus and Russia have free trade, imports of these goods continued to enter Russian territory tax free. Other specialized organizations, also created in 1993–94, such as the Afghan War Veterans' Union, continue to enjoy tax-exempt status. In 1995, the government established the Humanitarian Aid Commission, a body that may grant customs duty exemptions to organizations importing goods for humanitarian purposes. The scope of activities of the commission has expanded rapidly; in particular it has approved in a number of instances the importation of alcoholic beverages by religious and other organizations under the understanding that the proceeds of the sale of these beverages would be used for humanitarian ends. Once the tax-exempt status has been granted, however, there is no mechanism in place to check that the exemption is being used for the purposes originally intended. It is estimated that tax-exempt imports through the commission amount to several hundred million dollars a month.

Personal Income

(1) Excluded from the definition of taxable income are, among others, all types of pensions; all forms of severance pay; other benefits provided by the state; all interest income on bank deposits or other such instruments as well as interest earned on state bonds of the U.S.S.R.; income earned in gold prospecting, sand washing, casting, processing, and other activities related to gold production; income earned through the sale of apartments, houses, country houses, garden houses, land plots, and land shares (up to 5,000 minimum wages); income earned through the sale of animals (live or otherwise) as well as "products of plant and flower cultivation grown in natural or processed form";

amounts paid by enterprises to compensate employers for the cost of passes for children to establishments "for the leisure of parents with children"; income earned through the sale of willow bark, wild berries, nuts and other fruits, mushrooms, and medicinal herbs.

(2) The legislation also provides a number of additional exemptions, up to a predetermined level, typically set as a multiple of the minimum wage. For instance, war veterans may deduct from their monthly income the equivalent of five minimum wages.

(3) In addition, all military personnel and personnel attached to the security ministries and to other organs of state security, including the State Customs Committee, are exempt from paying any income tax at all.

IV Public Expenditure Reform

As part of its gradual move toward establishing a market economy based on the rule of law, Russia has scaled down significantly the size and scope of the public sector and has redefined the state's role as primary producer, allocator, and distributor in the economy. The period 1992–96 has witnessed a sustained reduction in the expenditure to GDP ratio that—for the consolidated government—fell from some 67 percent in 1992 to 38 percent in 1994 and to some 32 percent in 1996.[27] The reduction in federal expenditures has been especially pronounced, from 56 percent of GDP in 1992 to 24 percent in 1994 and to some 18½ percent in 1995–96, thus accounting for all of the total contraction (Table 7). On the whole, by 1996, expenditures at the federal level were dominated by debt service, defense and security, and various "protected" items with relatively limited discretion, while expenditures at the regional level were mainly accounted for by housing and other communal services, health, and education.

Coverage and Classification Issues

Analysis of the evolution of government operations is complicated by a number of changes in the structure of the budget that have significantly affected the coverage of expenditures. Official budget execution data for 1992 shows consolidated expenditures of some 33 percent of GDP and a deficit of just under 4 percent of GDP, figures that would appear at first sight to suggest both the relatively small size of the public sector in Russia in relation to that of other countries in Central and Eastern Europe and the restrained stance of fiscal policy. In reality, it reflects the fact that in the early stages of the transition many large operations were simply not included in the budget. During 1993–95 a number of quasi-fiscal

and credit operations previously off-budget were gradually incorporated into the budget.

Until mid-1993, the official budget did not fully account for foreign exchange revenues and expenditures. On the expenditure side, in particular, outlays on foreign currency debt (including to residents), centralized imports, and various foreign exchange allocations to ministries and other agencies were incorporated in the budget only insofar as they were financed by ruble allocations. Other expenditures, such as those financed by sales of gold and precious metals or foreign credits, were also not covered in the budget. Although attempts were made to include these expenditures (the inclusion of the equivalent of 12 percentage points of GDP in import subsidies in the expenditure data for 1992 is a good example of this), the coverage remained incomplete mainly because of the lack of systematic and comprehensive accounting of such operations. For instance, because of inadequate information, large balances on escrow accounts abroad to pay for centralized imports and financed by a share of the foreign exchange surrendered by exporters and certain export taxes were not included in more comprehensive versions of the government's operations.

A range of quasi-fiscal or net lending operations, some guaranteed by the Ministry of Finance, others in the form of directed credits by the central bank to the enterprise sector and which had not been included in the budget in 1992–93, gradually began to be incorporated in subsequent years as the scope of the underlying operations was reduced significantly. Such examples include (1) credits for the indexation of working capital (of the order of 3 percent of GDP in 1992); (2) credits to the Commonwealth of Independent States (CIS), mainly in the form of central bank correspondent accounts and technical credits amounting to over 8 percent of GDP in 1992; (3) credits to agriculture, to support planting and sowing in the spring and harvesting later in the year, a share of which began to be included in the budget as loans in mid-1994; (4) credits to the Northern Territories, incorporated in 1995; and (5) credits to support electric power generation in the Far East and purchases of fuel in the winter, among many others.

---

[27]These ratios exclude the operations of the extrabudgetary funds that, in relation to GDP, fell from some 12 percent of GDP in 1992 to about 9 percent in 1996, mainly because of a contraction in the expenditures of the Pension Fund.

Table 7. Government Expenditure
(In percent of GDP)

	1992	1993	1994	1995	1996
Expenditures at federal level[1]	55.9	27.8	24.3	17.6	19.8
National economy[2]	6.1	2.8	2.9	2.2	1.6
Education	1.3	0.8	0.9	0.5	0.5
Public health	0.3	0.3	0.4	0.4	0.4
Culture, arts, and mass media	0.3	0.2	0.3	0.2	0.1
Social protection	0.8	0.4	0.4	0.2	0.4
Science	0.6	0.5	0.5	0.3	...
Defense	4.7	4.4	4.4	2.9	2.8
Law enforcement	1.3	1.6	1.7	1.2	1.3
Administration	0.2	0.4	0.6	1.0	...
Intergovernmental transfers	1.8	2.7	3.5	1.5	2.3
Interest payments	0.8	2.1	1.9	3.4	5.6
Net lending[3]	3.7	1.7	2.2	1.4	0.9
Other	3.3	2.6	2.3	2.4	...
Unbudgeted import subsidies	11.9	2.3	—	—	—
Transfers to CIS states	8.5	2.0	—	—	—
Central bank directed credits[4]	15.5	5.0	2.3	—	—
Working capital transfers	3.3	—	—	—	—
Expenditures at regional level	13.0	17.0	17.5	14.5	14.7
National economy[5]	5.3	7.3	7.2	5.9	...
Education	2.5	3.5	3.5	2.9	3.2
Public health	2.3	3.0	2.8	2.3	2.3
Culture, arts, and mass media	0.3	0.4	0.5	0.4	
Social protection[6]	0.3	0.8	1.0	1.0	1.2
Law enforcement	0.4	0.1	0.1	0.4	...
Administration	0.4	0.5	0.5	0.4	...
Net lending	0.2	0.4	0.3	0.4	...
Other	1.3	1.0	1.6	0.8	...
Consolidated expenditures[7]	67.1	42.1	38.3	30.6	32.2
Memorandum item:					
GDP (in trillions of rubles)	18	172	611	1,630	2,256

Sources: Ministry of Finance; World Bank; and IMF staff estimates.

[1]Including unbudgeted import subsidies, central bank directed credits and working capital transfers, but excluding transfers to other CIS states.

[2]Includes subsidies to industry, energy, construction, agriculture, fishing, compensation for "price differences," capital investments, maintenance, among others.

[3]Credits for investment and industrial reconversion and other budgetary loans.

[4]To agriculture, fuel and energy, industry, the Northern Territories, among others.

[5]Includes subsidies for housing and utilities.

[6]Includes children's allowances.

[7]Net of intergovernmental transfers.

Various extrabudgetary funds were created at the federal and regional levels, particularly during 1991–92. In addition to the social funds (see Section V), various industrial and sectoral funds were also established, financed by a share of production costs and with the aim of furthering "investment and research and development." While no information is available on the number of these funds at the regional and local levels, it is estimated that at the federal level there were at least 50 in operation, collecting about 2–3 percent of GDP in revenue, all of it deductible from the profit tax base.

Apart from the issues of the appropriate coverage of budgetary expenditures, certain aspects of the classification of expenditures further complicate analysis of trends and sharply limit the usefulness of budget expenditure data. Budgetary expenditures are classified according to functional rather than economic criteria. The main categories of expenditure still reflect the main sectors of the economy as envisaged in the earlier national plans—such as sociocultural activities, defense, science, and national economy—with each category including both current and capital outlays (not separately identified) and sometimes consolidating large resources in a highly aggregated fashion. Although a new system of budgetary classification was introduced with the 1995 budget, which lists expenditures by government function, economic characteristics, and spending units, no economic classification for the 1995 outturn is yet available.[28]

Composition

As shown in Table 8, subsidies (budgeted and unbudgeted) during 1992 amounted to about 26 percent of GDP and consisted mainly of subsidies to agriculture, the coal industry, military conversion projects, interest payments, and imports, as well as some other amounts provided through local budgets. The most important of these were import subsidies associated with purchases of commodities through the budget under the centralized imports scheme and those linked to tied foreign credits involving the resale by the government of commodities (grain, spare parts, medicines, and processed food) financed by external loans at prices that implied a large subsidy element. The latter type were not included in the budget; the combination of the two was equivalent to 15 percent of GDP in 1992, with the bulk (12 percent of GDP) corresponding to the unbudgeted type. The rate of effective subsidization for various commodities (given by the difference between the market price implied by the prevailing exchange rate and the ruble counterpart actually collected from the receiving enterprise) varied over time but was generally in the range of 90–100 percent. An additional 11 percent of GDP was provided through various consumer and producer subsidies. Consumer subsidies took the form of price subsidies for a number of food items, medicines, heating, and rent and transportation, with the latter provided through local budgets. Price liberalization notwithstanding, local governments continued to monitor closely the prices of essential food items and provided direct consumer subsidies, as needed and as dictated by the availability of resources and local prerogatives. This practice, to a greater or lesser degree, remained in force for the next several years in a large number of regions. De facto then, during 1992, there was a significant shift in expenditure responsibilities to the local level for

Table 8. Subsidies to the Economy in 1992
(In billions of rubles)

	1992
1. Nonimport subsidies	1,384
(In percent of GDP)	(7.7)
Coal industry	180
Agriculture	344
Of which:	
Livestock	163
Farmers' Fund	54
Producer subsidies	114
Military conversion	130
Local budgets	585
Interest subsidies[1]	115
Other subsidies	30
2. Import-related subsidies	2,721
(In percent of GDP)	15.0
Budgeted	576
Unbudgeted	2,145
3. Other subsidies	650
4. Total subsidies (1+2+3)	4,755
(In percent of GDP)	(26.3)
Coal subsidy	1.0
Agricultural	1.9
Military conversion	0.7
Total interest subsidy[2]	0.6
From local budgets	3.2
Total import subsidies	15.0
Other subsidies	3.6
GDP (in trillions of rubles)	18.1

Sources: Ministry of Finance; and IMF staff estimates.
[1]To Rosselkhosbank and Northern Territories.
[2]Through the Farmers' Fund and commercial banks and excluding quasi-fiscal operations associated with interest payments on directed credits.

the subsidization of essential items. In the aggregate, regional housing and utilities subsidies amounted to 3–4 percent of GDP in 1995–96.

Producer subsidies were mainly provided to agriculture and the coal industry. Subsidies to agriculture took the form of allocations for the improvement of agricultural land, for livestock production, to compensate for "high" energy costs, for housing construction, and to offset the "high" cost of borrowing, the latter typically provided so as to reduce the effective interest rate to a fraction of the central bank refinance rate. Those to the coal industry consisted of wage subsidies and direct subsidies to finance social expenditures. In addition, industrial and agricultural enterprises received interest rate subsidies on central-bank-directed credits amounting to some 3 percent of GDP, to cover the difference between the central

---

[28]For a fuller discussion of these issues, see the section on Budget Process and Institutional Reform below.

bank refinance rate and the interest paid by enterprises to commercial banks. In 1992, directed credits amounted to some 19 percent of GDP, both from the central bank and the government, the latter through working capital injections equivalent to some 3½ percent of GDP. Since the bulk of these directed credits (and additional amounts disbursed in 1993–94) are not expected to be repaid, it may be more appropriate to think of them as grants, given to finance the provision of social benefits and services, to continue in an indirect way to provide some degree of consumer subsidization, and to finance capital flight.[29]

Much progress was made during the transition period in eliminating the bulk of such subsidies through the emergence of a more transparent system of resource allocation. As price liberalization led to a more rational structure of signals and incentives in the economy, the extent of the prevailing distortions became glaringly evident. By 1993 and in the context of a unified exchange rate, import subsidies had been sharply curtailed, amounting to no more than 2½ percent of GDP for the year as a whole; indeed, the reduction in the fiscal deficit that year is mainly accounted for by a drop of nearly 10 percentage points of GDP in unbudgeted subsidies. Progress in eliminating other subsidies was considerably slower but, against the magnitude of the underlying distortions, made some headway. The move to a market-based system of interest rate determination allowed for a more transparent accounting of the interest cost associated with subsidizing activities in the enterprise sector, particularly in agriculture. While interest rate subsidies continued to be provided through the period under review, these were increasingly limited in scale and aimed at a relatively small number of activities, mainly in the agricultural sector. For instance, the 1995 budget identified four major areas as recipients of budgetary loans at a fraction of the central bank refinance rate: investment programs and defense industry conversion (one-fourth of the central bank refinance rate); supplies to the Northern Territories (one-third); purchases of agricultural products for the Federal Food Funds (one-third); and the Federal Fund for Fuel Procurement (one-third). It should be noted, however, that although the bulk of new lending to agriculture was at market rates, a large share of the loans was rolled over and little interest was actually collected.[30]

The difficulties in compressing expenditure significantly beyond the levels implied by the elimination of subsidies and other obviously inefficient expenditure items have been apparent in other economies in transition; indeed, in some of these countries (such as Poland and Hungary) the total expenditure to GDP ratios were higher in 1992, two years after the onset of the transition, than in 1990. It is interesting to compare the evolution of selected components of expenditure (especially current expenditure) in several of the transition economies in Eastern Europe with those in Russia. As Figure 6 shows, spending on wages and salaries and interest payments rose significantly relative to pretransition levels. The increase over the four-year period beginning one year before the implementation of the authorities' most comprehensive economic reform program and ending two years later shows an average combined rise in these two components of expenditure of some 4–5 percentage points of GDP. The rise mainly reflects liberalization of interest rate policy and the subsequent emergence of positive real interest rates, together with growing borrowing from domestic and foreign financial markets, and wage policies intended to prevent a massive shift of qualified personnel to the rapidly growing private sector, as well as the monetization of in-kind benefits.[31] In Russia, as in other countries, interest payments in relation to GDP also rose in response to the liberalization of interest rates and the move away from subsidized directed central bank credits toward market-related debt instruments (see the section Budget Financing below).

Producer subsidies fell sharply in all transition countries and, in general, the larger the drop the more pronounced was the corresponding fall in industrial output, since the bulk of these subsidies was allocated to industrial enterprises. As noted earlier, cutbacks in producer subsidies adversely affected the financial position of enterprises and contributed to less ambitious investment plans and production, layoffs, and tax and payments arrears. Purchases of goods and services and capital spending fell across all of these countries. The declines were especially pronounced in Bulgaria and Romania (not shown in Figure 6; in Romania capital expenditure fell from 18 percent of GDP in 1989 to 6 percent in 1992).

---

[29]Directed credits from the central bank in 1992 amounted to roughly $14 billion.

[30]For instance, Government Resolution No. 126 of February 23, 1994, on measures "to assist the agricultural complex," instructs the Credit Policy Commission and the central bank to allocate during the first half of 1994 "no less than Rub 5 trillion" (0.8 percent of GDP) in directed credits to agricultural enterprises for the purchase of various inputs for the spring sowing season. The

resolution also instructs the central bank to grant these credits with a maturity of "up to three years" and explicitly defers payment of principal and interest until September 1, at which point it is expected that farmers would have the resources to begin to pay their loans. The Ministry of Finance was also instructed to continue to finance in 1994 the interest rate differential on preferential credits granted to certain categories of farmers during 1992 and 1993; the bulk of these credits was granted at 28 percent.

[31]It is noteworthy that, notwithstanding this rise, wages and salaries in transition economies remain well below levels in Western industrial economies.

Figure 6. Selected Countries: Government Expenditure by Components[1]
(In percent of GDP)

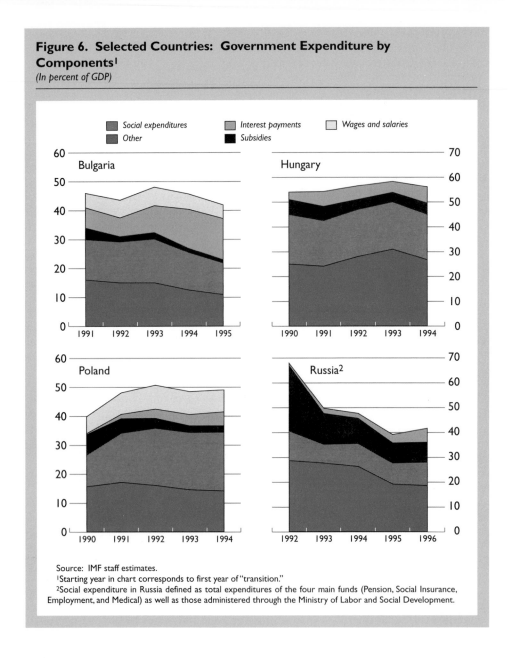

Source: IMF staff estimates.
[1]Starting year in chart corresponds to first year of "transition."
[2]Social expenditure in Russia defined as total expenditures of the four main funds (Pension, Social Insurance, Employment, and Medical) as well as those administered through the Ministry of Labor and Social Development.

Expenditures in the form of income transfers (consumer subsidies plus social expenditures) went up in all transition countries, with the fall in subsidies being more than offset by the rise in expenditures; the increases in social expenditures in Poland in 1990–92 were particularly high (9 percentage points of GDP), mainly in the form of increases in pensions and unemployment benefits. These increases were intended to offset declines in real wages and in income from consumer subsidies following price liberalization. In 1992–96, transition countries made limited progress in improving the efficiency of social spending. In contrast, in Russia, as noted earlier, consumer subsidies were reduced significantly and social expenditures fell simultaneously. In relation to GDP, social expenditures carried out by the social funds (pensions, unemployment compensation, and social benefits provided through the Social Insurance Fund, among others) fell by some 3 percentage points of GDP between 1992 and 1996.[32]

---

[32]For a more detailed discussion of social issues, see Section V.

Scope for Additional Expenditure Compression

One argument often made in Russia about the limited scope for a further reduction in the size and the functions of the public sector is that, once the most apparent inefficiencies and distortions are eliminated, particularly subsidies, areas will remain where significant spending may be necessary. A number of observations can be made in this regard. First, while it is true that many of the institutions of the centralized economy have been eliminated, such as planning and price offices, branch ministries, and so on, new ones have been created or will need to be created to oversee previously nonexisting activities, such as privatization, bank regulation and supervision, and tax policing. Others will need to be strengthened considerably to be able to deal effectively with expanded functions and responsibilities in the context of an emerging market economy. A key example would be the State Tax Service, given the large increase in the number of taxpayers. Likewise, while some of the functions of state security agencies have been phased out in the context of building up democratic institutions in Russia and greater awareness of the importance of basic human rights, there are important needs in the fight against a rising tide of crime, which is a fundamental concern of the population. There will be growing needs in the judicial area as well, as efforts continue to establish the rule of law and, as a result, more cases are settled through the courts. It may not be feasible nor desirable, therefore, to compress further expenditures that directly finance essential functions of the state in a modern economy (see Table 9).[33] Furthermore, pressures for expenditures in other areas will also continue. Some of the more important of these are examined below.

Interest payments. In a context of high real interest rates and still relatively short maturities, payment pressures will continue, given the accumulation of public debt associated with budget deficits and the increasing use of market-based debt instruments to finance budgetary shortfalls. There are two aspects to this. The first is the level of interest payments (including on external debt), which have grown rapidly in recent years to more than 5 percent of GDP in 1996. The other pertains to the need to nurture growing confidence in Russia's financial system against a backdrop of disruptions such as confiscatory "monetary reforms" (for example, under the Pavlov government, 1991), bankrupcies (Vneshekonombank, affecting over $10 billion of foreign currency deposits of residents, 1991), and old/new ruble swaps (1993), all of which undermined public trust and contributed to the high premiums being demanded for the holding of treasury bills and other debt instruments. Yet another aspect of this is the budgetary cost of bank recapitalization through government bond issues. Since a share of the loan portfolio of Russia's banks may be nonperforming, some systemwide solution may be warranted that could entail significant yearly interest costs.

Wages. Wages will come under pressure as various hidden subsidies at the enterprise level continue to be eliminated (housing, some forms of social protection, and so on) and also to narrow the gap with the private sector and, more generally, with Russia's main trade partners. The average monthly wage in the public sector in 1994–95 was equivalent to some 50–75 percent of the average wage for the economy.[34]

Capital spending. To stem the further deterioration of physical infrastructure and of the health and education systems, both of which have come under heavy strain during the transition, capital spending will rise. Neither of these categories of expenditure can be neglected, given the development lessons of the past two decades about the future economic costs of inattention to them. It is by now well accepted that the economic returns to investment in education and health "are often extremely high" and that the economy's future growth potential will be undermined by the prolonged disregard of these two sectors.[35] In addition, experience in other countries has shown that a deteriorated transport and communications infrastructure can be an important deterrent to foreign direct investment. Significant environmental cleanup will also be necessary, given the unfortunate legacy of disregard for Russia's habitat. This is particularly the case as regards the safe disposal of nuclear waste (of which Russia has a large world share) and the deactivation of a number of nuclear power facilities, many of which are associated with the military-industrial complex. There are justifiable concerns that inattention to these issues poses considerable risks for the environment, in some cases on a regional scale. There is also broad consensus that such cleanup is extremely costly and must be carried out over a long-term horizon.

Industrial reconversion. Some form of industrial reconversion will continue, particularly in the military. Industrial activity in Russia has contracted sharply in the past several years (a cumulative drop in industrial production of 53 percent over 1991–96 and affecting every sector from electric power gener-

---

[33]The table provides a listing of general government expenditure levels in OECD member countries.

[34] Average real wages in the public sector (federal level) fell by 40 percent during 1995.

[35]See Summers and Thomas (1993, p. 245).

Table 9. Selected Countries: General Government Expenditures
(In percent of GDP)

	1985	1991	1992	1993	1994	1995	1996
Canada	45.3	49.2	50.2	49.4	47.1	46.5	44.7
Germany	47.0	47.9	48.5	49.5	48.9	49.5	49.0
France	52.1	50.4	52.0	54.6	54.0	53.9	54.5
Italy	51.2	53.7	56.3	57.1	54.8	52.1	52.9
United Kingdom	44.0	40.7	43.1	43.5	43.1	43.2	41.9
United States	32.9	33.4	34.4	33.9	33.0	33.2	33.3
Belgium	61.6	55.7	56.2	57.1	55.7	55.0	54.3
Denmark	59.3	59.2	61.1	63.8	64.0	61.1	61.5
Netherlands	57.2	54.6	55.1	55.2	53.0	52.2	49.9
Finland	43.8	53.9	59.1	60.2	59.3	58.3	57.4
Spain	41.2	43.4	44.4	47.7	45.9	44.8	43.3
Sweden	63.3	61.3	67.2	71.0	68.3	66.4	64.7
European Union countries	49.0	48.8	50.4	51.9	50.8	50.2	49.8
OECD countries	38.9	39.3	40.5	41.1	40.3	40.3	40.3

Source: Organization for Economic Cooperation and Development, *Economic Outlook,* June 1997.

ation—21 percent—to light manufactures—87 percent), owing to a broad range of factors. These include excess capacity in the military-industrial complex that had evolved in the past on the basis of certain assumptions about the likely evolution of the international political climate, assumptions that proved to be wrong; inefficient pricing policies; overmanning; delays in the modernization of the capital stock (an especially important consideration in the energy sector); excessive growth of labor costs in the pretransition period and an unusually elastic budget constraint that did not prepare the enterprise sector for the more competitive environment brought about by price and trade liberalization. A process aimed at restoring enterprises' balance sheets in those enterprises in which government participation is likely to remain high (for example, within the military-industrial complex), is likely to entail significant financial costs.

Beyond this, there remains the problem of the Closed Administrative Territorial Units, a list of 40 cities officially recognized by the federal budget as being centers for "specialized military production." With an average population of some 200,000 inhabitants, these cities are fully supported by the federal budget, mainly in the form of subsistence level wages and subsidies. Because they are typically far from other urban centers and because of the exclusively military nature of their production, it is unlikely that these cities will be economically viable. They will thus continue to be a drain on the budget and, to the extent that they represent unused re-

sources, a drain on the economy as well. The development of a medium-term strategy to close many of them, to finance the migration of their inhabitants to other regions, and to restructure and modernize some of the production facilities will also entail financial costs. In addition, the government will also have to meet some of the costs associated with the reconstruction of Chechnya, particularly in the area of infrastructure.

Social assistance. The financing of social assistance in general (see Section V for further discussion) will continue. This will include the financing of unemployment compensation and the selective transfer to the budget of some of the social functions presently performed by the enterprise sector, a process that, although costly, is itself an important component of the transition to a market economy. Indeed, Tanzi (1993b, p. 5) has argued that an undue focus on the budget deficit as a measure of macroeconomic performance "that ignores this transfer might be met by the government delaying the transfer of these social functions from the enterprises to the budget." This would undermine rather than enhance the transition. All the above are likely to exert upward pressure on budgetary expenditures over the medium term.

Tanzi's point warrants further comment. He notes that focusing on the conventionally measured budget deficit (as opposed to a comprehensive and economically meaningful measure of the fiscal deficit that might include such items as social expenditures carried out by the enterprise sector and that, in market economies, are typically the responsibility of the state, or cheap loans and other quasi-fiscal operations) may create perverse incentives by inducing the government to adopt policies that go against other key elements of the transition. Some examples with respect to Russia would be (1) the unwillingness of the government to improve the level and coverage of unemployment compensation that has resulted in continued labor hoarding at the enterprise level, notwithstanding the large output drops; (2) subsidized credit by the central bank that during 1992–94 greatly reduced the cost of debt service by the government; and (3) the shifting of expenditures out of the budget to extrabudgetary accounts.

Budget Process and Institutional Reform

As in other countries in transition, a redefinition of the role of the public sector may be called for, from one largely focused on control and direction to one of supporting the private sector through the further freeing of market forces and the establishment of a simple regulatory framework based on transparent rules. The Russian economy needs to be freed from excessive intervention, arbitrary decisions, and the inconsistent application of rules and policies, all of which are likely to hinder business activity and slow the pace of private sector investment.[36] The adjustment process in Russia has sometimes been undermined by weaknesses in the government's administrative capacities, underscoring the need for ambitious institutional reforms. A case can be made that the effectiveness of adjustment policies will depend in no small measure on the extent to which they are supported by policies aimed at improving the institutional setup on which sustained implementation ultimately rests. The freeing up of prices, for instance, will encourage a supply response but its magnitude is likely to be larger in the context of adequate infrastructure for transport and credit institutions that allocate resources relatively efficiently. Adequate legal underpinnings and a framework for public accountability are also key elements of institution-building reforms. In all these processes, the role of the government is critical and must be geared to the efficient management of economic policy, facilitating the transition to better policies and the design and implementation of structural and institutional reforms.

Because of their central role in the implementation of fiscal policy, reforms are urgently needed in the formulation and execution of the budget. A review of the experience with the elaboration of the budget since 1990 shows that no two years have been alike. Budgetary procedures have changed significantly each year linked to changes in the economic and political environment. This section discusses budgetary procedures for the 1995 and 1996 budgets, as these contain the key elements that are likely to remain in place over the medium term. A number of serious weaknesses are also identified and possible solutions suggested.

The Ministry of Finance plays the central coordinating role in the budgetary process. Work on the following year's budget begins with the issuing of a government resolution (*postanovlenie*) on the preparation of the budget, which contains various deadlines for the submission of information necessary for the elaboration of the budget to the Ministry of Finance by all the various spending ministries and agencies (henceforth referred to as "spending units"). The Ministry of Economy is asked to prepare a basic macroeconomic scenario, which forms the basis of the budget calculations. This mainly involves the setting of an inflation target for the year for which the budget is being prepared together with the quarterly inflation profile as well as "wage coefficients" that are to be applied to estimate the wage bill through the year on a quarter-by-quarter basis. Following the issuing of this resolution, there is usually a brief discussion between the staffs of the Ministry of Finance and the Ministry of Economy on the adequacy of the targets underlying the Ministry of Economy's scenario, and shortly thereafter these estimates are sent to all spending units expected to submit spending requests to the Ministry of Finance.[37] Major progress has been made in recent years in starting the budgetary exercise early, to prevent situations such as those that prevailed until 1994, when the final budget for that year was approved only in June, which meant that spending units did not know the final level of appropriations until that time and thus could not adequately plan or commit resources.

The Ministry of Finance asks spending units for forecasts of their individual budgetary execution through the end of the year as well as a list of their

---

[36]There is much international evidence, for instance, that a strong disincentive to foreign investment is the presence of an inconsistent and complex set of signals, subject to a high degree of uncertainty. Investment decisions involve issues of long-range planning; from the investor's perspective a well-identified, simple, and stable set of rules—even if somewhat restrictive—may be preferable to one perceived to be opaque and subject to unpredictable changes.

---

[37]Occasionally, at the time that these estimates are sent, other supporting materials may also be forwarded to all the spending units. For the 1995 budget, for instance, the Ministry of Finance sent an explanatory note on the new system of budgetary classification.

demands for the following year. This exercise allows for drawing up an "unchanged policies" base for the current year from which to make forecasts for the year for which the budget is being prepared. At the time the spending units prepare their individual current-year forecasts, they may also include any extraordinary or unanticipated expenditure requests arising, for instance, from recent spending decisions made by the executive that they feel they are obliged to cover, legislation that may have been approved recently that could have an impact upon their individual units' spending behavior during the following period (for example, unforeseen adjustments in the previous year's wage coefficients) or, more generally, new spending they regard as essential for the implementation of the functions under their jurisdiction. Upon receipt of this information, the Ministry of Finance will instruct the spending units what expenditure items to exclude from the projected base and will provide information on the areas that are more likely to be financed; the aim of this is to work with as realistic a base for the current year as possible. This will typically involve cuts even in areas that may be part of the officially approved budget for the current year, given the shortfalls in revenue that have been a permanent feature of budgetary implementation in recent years. The figures provided by the spending units to the Ministry of Finance will typically consist of base-year forecasts multiplied by an appropriate array of price and wage coefficients. They will also include a listing of all new expenditures, separately identified and justified, particularly for those involving new decisions. While this work at a disaggregated level goes on, the Ministry of Finance prepares a detailed revenue forecast, identifies additional sources of financing, and sets limits on the budget deficit.

In 1993–95 the initial set of demands submitted by the over 100 spending units typically were somewhere between two to three times higher than the sum of revenues plus identified financing. This is the point at which the Ministry of Finance's most difficult task begins, the ultimate aim of which is to match spending authorizations within the budget with the sources of revenue and additional financing, consistent with the targeted deficit. With the sharp deceleration of inflation in 1995/96 and the emergence of medium-term fiscal deficit targets, it is thought that the initial gap between resources requested and resources ultimately approved could be narrowed somewhat.

There are typically three stages to the above negotiation. To more easily identify the nature of the discussions, an illustrative example may be useful. In the first stage, the Department of the Social Sphere in the Ministry of Finance will meet with representatives from the Financial Department of, say, the Ministry of Culture. This ministry's requests will be discussed and a compromise will be attempted trying to reconcile the needs of the ministry with the overall expenditure and deficit targets worked out by the Ministry of Finance. Full compromises are seldom reached at this stage, although the gaps are usually narrowed. These discussions will then be followed by a round of meetings between the Budgetary Department of the Ministry of Finance and other divisions with primary responsibility for different areas of the economy within the ministry—social sphere, industrial production, agriculture, and so on—at which a second round of cuts will be made to bring the aggregate requests emanating from the first stage down to a level that is more consistent with the Ministry of Finance's targets. Finally, at a third stage, the Minister of Culture himself or some high-ranking official from that ministry will come to the Ministry of Finance and will meet with either the Minister or, more typically, a Deputy Minister of Finance, to make a case against some of the cuts that may have been proposed by the Ministry of Finance but that the Ministry of Culture is simply not ready to accept. At this last stage, the Ministry of Finance will typically provide the Ministry of Culture with the upper limits of expenditure consistent with the deficit target and the available sources of financing, although many of the spending units will reserve for themselves the right to appeal these decisions to the next level of decision making (see below).

In recent years, these three stages have typically taken somewhere between three to four weeks, although it is expected that in the future the process will be longer. In the high inflation environment of 1993–95, when the budget process was initially delayed and the budget itself was revised several times in the course of the year, the Ministry of Finance was under great pressure to present a budget to the government, a situation that did not permit a more considered view of spending priorities (see below).

Following this last round of negotiations and during a two- to three-week period, the Ministry of Finance will consolidate all spending units' allocations into an aggregate budget. It will draft explanatory notes, prepare tables, and submit a first draft of the budget to the government. This is typically done by the Minister of Finance and some of his deputies meeting with the Prime Minister to report on the results of the exercise and to identify for him the salient features of the budget and spending priorities, indicating also those areas where the most significant "cuts" were made and what some of the possible risks could be in cutting down the spending units' initial expenditure requests to more reasonable levels. At this stage, the Prime Minister may raise questions, including requesting additional information on the relative share of spending allocated to each unit, the increase with respect to the previous year, the extent of the cuts made and areas where these may have been made, and so on.

When the budget is presented to the Prime Minister, there will typically be an unallocated reserve equivalent to 3–5 percent of total revenue. At this stage, the Prime Minister will allocate this reserve fully to those units that he may feel were perhaps unduly cut or where the ministry itself may have felt a plausible case could be made for some additional spending. These discussions with the Prime Minister will typically take no more than about a week. Immediately thereafter the Prime Minister will present the draft budget to the government at a meeting of the Cabinet. At this meeting, many ministers will raise objections and typically argue that the interests of their respective sectors are being adversely affected by the large cuts they are being asked to sustain with respect to their initial demands. Ahead of this meeting considerable time will have been spent by each agency preparing papers and explaining (sometimes in great detail) the well-justified nature of their demands. The experience in the last two budgetary exercises has been that, notwithstanding the entreaties made by ministers at the Cabinet meeting, no fundamental changes were made to the proposals submitted by the Ministry of Finance. The essential problem has been that while all would like to have more resources to spend, the new sources of additional financing are not always clear. Given government reluctance to move more aggressively on the revenue front (as noted earlier, the government itself has often taken initiatives that have undermined revenue collection) and since, at this point, the size of the deficit is typically not negotiable, there is little, if any, room to accommodate such expenditure requests.

One of the main weaknesses at this stage of the budgetary process is that the Ministry of Finance is given the responsibility of negotiating with the spending units without having a clear understanding of the nature of their operations. Negotiations on expenditure cuts are often conducted in a vacuum of relevant data that might allow better informed choices. To go back to the example of the Ministry of Culture, the following situation might occur. The Ministry of Culture was able in previous budgetary exercises to obtain financing for the purchase of art works and other inputs for a number of important museums. These purchases were carried out, as budgeted, but, say, no such expenditures are necessary in the budget for 1997. However, it may well be that the Ministry of Culture submits a request for additional acquisitions so as not to lose the budgetary allocation given in earlier exercises, although, in fact, no such acquisitions are expected in the forthcoming fiscal year, or not to the extent requested. Because

the negotiation is made with the Ministry of Finance at a very aggregate level, the aim of which is to try to compress expenditures down to a level consistent with the overall macroeconomic aggregates, little attention is paid to the individual structure of expenditure within each of the spending units. Consequently, the Ministry of Finance often finds itself in the position of not knowing whether the cuts it eventually enforces on the Ministry of Culture are leaving that ministry underfinanced or overfinanced, whether they are leading to an extremely difficult and inefficient situation—in terms of the overall interests of the economy—or whether because of earlier "creative accounting" on the part of an individual spending unit they are, in fact, leaving it in a relatively comfortable position and are, therefore, imposing costs on other spending units where no such accounting took place and where perhaps the proposals were more transparent at the outset.

The absence of long time series on selected expenditure items for the spending units, the inflationary environment in which the budgetary exercises have thus far taken place—which made two- or threefold increases in nominal expenditures seem "reasonable," shortages of qualified staff at the Ministry of Finance who might follow up, over time, spending behavior in some of the key spending units and make ex post comparisons between "approved" and "actual" expenditures, all contribute to make the exercise extremely inefficient, potentially unfair, and liable to abuse. Incremental budgeting in a high-inflation transition economy poses certain risks that demand special vigilance on the part of the authorities. High inflation may give an aura of legitimacy to requests for higher nominal spending at a time when the transition itself may require the government to withdraw from certain traditional areas of financing. Identifying those areas, deciding how best to allocate scarce resources, and deciding where cuts will best serve the interests of economic efficiency require considerable administrative capacity that needs to be developed as a key priority of economic management.

Following the Cabinet meeting the government sends the budget to the Duma. The Duma will typically analyze the budget in considerable detail over two to four weeks. At its first hearing, it may either approve or reject the budget as a whole. Approval of the budget on the first reading implies acceptance of the underlying macroeconomic assumptions and other basic assumptions that may have been included in the preparation of the budget—for instance, "no monetary financing in 1995." If it is rejected, it is typically sent back to the government with various comments and requests.

Or alternatively, the Duma, as was the case for the 1995 and subsequent budgets, may decide to appoint an interagency Conciliatory Commission to try to bring consensus to the large body of different opinions that will have formed on the appropriateness of the budgetary stance proposed by the Ministry of Finance and the government. Typically these are the most detailed discussions on the budget and will involve a number of different committees within the Duma, the Ministry of Finance, the central bank, and various spending units. Following approval of the budget at the first reading, the second reading will involve approval of the revenue, expenditure, and deficit aggregate figures. At the third reading, individual items of revenue and expenditure are discussed, with the emphasis on the latter, often involving significant additional reallocation within the various expenditure chapters. The fourth and final reading is a general discussion at which the Duma also approves such aspects of the budget as external financing proposals and fiscal federalism issues.

It is important to emphasize that at the time of the second reading when the aggregate parameters of the budget are discussed and approved there is not a great deal of scope for boosting revenue given that in the first reading the Duma has already approved the macroeconomic assumptions underlying the budget and, in particular, the price and wage forecasts used in the entire exercise. This has not prevented the Duma, however, from inflating revenues, often significantly, in every budget exercise during the past several years, increases that are then allocated to various spending categories. A variant to this (for example, the 1996 and 1997 budgets) involves the Ministry of Finance presenting overly optimistic revenue estimates at the outset that, ex post, give the government considerable sequestration discretion when, inevitably, revenues fall short (see below).

One of the weakest points in this process is the lack of an effective linkage between such additional revenue "requests" on the one hand and the necessary underlying tax legislation on the other, often with no attempt being made by the Duma to formalize the linkage that exists between the two. For instance, the Duma will "find" alternative sources of revenue (usually motivated by pressures for additional spending) but will not follow through with the necessary legislation that will make it possible to collect that additional revenue. This, therefore, creates a "reality gap" that leads to the overestimation of revenues by as much as 10–20 percent. A case in point: the Duma identifies Rub X trillion of additional revenue by proposing the elimination of certain import duty exemptions for a particular group of organizations. It allocates the additional revenue that is generated by the "elimination" of the exemptions to, say, defense expenditure, but then once the budget is approved it does not follow through with the appropriate legislative acts that might make it actually possible to eliminate the exemptions and collect

the revenue. In the meantime, however, the higher level of expenditure has been approved and an inconsistency is thus created between the reasonably carefully worked out proposals of the Ministry of Finance and the figures that are eventually approved and become part of the budget law. The government has often accepted this inconsistent approach as part of the strategy to "buy support" for the budget, for instance, from the agrarian lobby or other interest groups. However, this typically leads to a situation where the sum of actual revenues and financing turn out to be less than the levels anticipated in the budget, which creates problems for budgetary implementation. A similar situation arises as a result of the indexation of wages, including the minimum wage, and pensions. The principle is basically the same: a number of decisions are taken in the course of the year that were not fully anticipated in the budget eventually approved and that again create difficulties for implementation.

An additional source of "noise" in the system once the budget has been approved is the number of decrees or resolutions of the government and the executive that are issued practically on a daily basis and that typically involve additional spending. In some cases, the Ministry of Finance may claim that these decisions are, in fact, already incorporated in the budget. Again, an illustrative example might be that the Ministry of Culture has a budget approved for the construction of a new museum. A senior member of the government visits a particular town and promises the population and the local authorities to build a new museum for Rub X billion. The Ministry of Finance may subsequently claim that the museum promised was, in fact, already budgeted for and included in the original request of the Ministry of Culture, an observation unlikely to be appreciated by this ministry since they may have had an entirely different place in mind on which, even, work may already have commenced. The Ministry of Finance, however, may not always be able to do this because the promises made (or something resembling them) are nowhere to be found in the original budget proposals. In this case, the Ministry of Finance finds itself in the position of having to cut elsewhere. Obviously this creates imbalances; in the absence of additional revenues, departures with respect to "approved" spending paths are inevitable and the possibility of major inequities in the spending process is increased.

The opposite situation may be created when actual inflation is higher than that incorporated in the budget, leading to additional revenues that can facilitate the implementation of such promises, assuming that the additional revenues thus generated more than offset the adverse impact of overly optimistic baseline forecasts. It is estimated that "new promises" requiring spending cuts elsewhere after the budget has been approved amount to 5–10 percent of total expenditures.

When faced with lower-than-anticipated levels of financing (including lower revenues), the government is forced to cut expenditure accordingly, and for this purpose it has developed a number of guiding principles. Capital spending tends to be cut first. Current spending is typically cut across the board, although certain components, such as debt service, wages, stipends, and some items of a social nature are considered "protected" and thus, in theory, not subject to such cuts. In practice, however, these guidelines are not always adhered to. It may not be feasible to cut in the short term certain capital projects, and thus, for instance, wage arrears may build up. A considerable level of arbitrariness in the spending process is thus introduced. The spending authorizations included in the budget rapidly become no more than a loose framework providing spending units with an upper indicative limit for resources likely (or unlikely) to be received. Considerable uncertainty in their operations is thus created, and much time is then spent on deciding how to reallocate priorities within their (effectively) reduced level of spending and on lobbying the government for maintaining a certain flow of financing. Indeed, the larger the financing shortfall the more the activities of the spending units are turned into emergency cash management and lobbying operations.

On occasion, as it happened in August 1995, a particular spending unit (in this case, the Ministry of Defense) may unilaterally decide to carry out spending not authorized in the budget: for example, a 25 percent increase in the wages of the military amounting to some Rub 7 trillion (0.8 percent of GDP) for the last five months of the year, which is then validated by the government.[38] As in the earlier example, given the budget's overall deficit limits, such decisions force drastic cuts elsewhere, contributing to the emergence of situations where the budget at times is able to finance little beyond the payment of wages and interest on the public debt.

Sequestration inevitably contributes to the growth of arrears. Beyond those associated with the nonpayment of otherwise "authorized" spending, it creates an environment in which not meeting commitments is regarded by economic agents as tolerable behavior, including, of course, the payment of taxes to the budget. It greatly reduces the credibility of the budget as an instrument of fiscal policy and of the government as the chief architect of that policy. Fiscal policy, the elements of which, in most cases, govern-

ments tend to revise once a year on the occasion of the preparation of the budget, is then reduced to weekly and/or daily cash management mainly involving "who gets how much." Such an approach is enormously inefficient and detracts the authorities' attention from the kind of policy concerns and strategic planning and thinking that is essential in Russia, given the serious problems that remain, as noted in earlier sections. Since the above inefficiencies are precipitated, by and large, by revenue shortfalls, there is no alternative, over the medium term, to considerably improving revenue performance and tax administration. Alternatively, faced with tight deficit ceilings and financing shortfalls, the government may authorize spending units to borrow short term from commercial banks under government guarantees (not recorded in the budget), as begun to be made in the latter part of 1995 and continued in earnest in the course of 1996.

The experience of the past several years has shown that the structure of expenditures after the budget was implemented was radically different from that anticipated in the approved budget (Table 10). Spending units are obliged to present their expenditure plans to the Ministry of Finance following a system of economic classification but the distribution of expenditure is, in effect, purely indicative and no attempt is made later to compare the initial budget proposals with the figures actually executed (Figure 7). Since spending units will have typically received less than the budgeted amounts, the Ministry of Finance does not feel it has the authority to go back and verify discrepancies or departures with respect to initial plans. Indeed, in the course of the year, as resources become available, the Ministry of Finance will credit the accounts of the spending units, but there is no formal requirement that the resources received should be spent in a way that reflects the original proposals presented by the government and ultimately approved by the Duma (for example, x percent to wages and salaries, z percent to capital investment). If it becomes evident that resources received have been grossly misallocated, the Ministry of Finance may "inform" the government, but typically, no further action is taken. Furthermore, there are certain spending units (for example, the Ministry of Defense) for which the informational requirements associated with the uses of the resources allocated to them are considerably less stringent. In light of the above, it is perhaps not surprising that no time-series data exist, for instance, on the share of budgetary spending allocated to wages and salaries.[39] Indeed, no official budget execution data

---

[38]Indeed, this increase was not incorporated as part of the 1996 budget either, but was fully financed by the Ministry of Finance.

[39]It is estimated that 16 percent of total federal expenditure in 1996 was allocated to wages and salaries.

Table 10. Budgeted and Actual Federal Expenditures, 1994
(In percent of GDP)

	Budget	Actual
Total federal expenditure	31.0	22.0
National economy	7.2	3.0
Education, culture, arts, and public health	2.1	1.5
Science	0.8	0.5
Defense	6.4	4.4
Law enforcement	2.0	1.7
Intergovernmental transfers	4.3	3.5
Other	8.2	7.4

Source: Ministry of Finance.

around 16–20 percent), this inevitably forces sharp changes in the structure of budgetary spending. At the same time, shortfalls in foreign financing may also induce a restructuring of the budget as the budget is implemented. For this reason, because there are sizable differences between the structure of expenditures as approved and as actually implemented, the Duma has argued for shifting the elaboration of the budget to a quarterly basis in an attempt to have more control over spending; this has not been supported by the government. Reflecting the above discrepancy, the actual budget execution for the previous year has never been discussed in a session of the Duma. There seems to be agreement that, as long as the deficiencies are not corrected, such debate would not be especially useful and might, by highlighting the underlying weaknesses, actually further undermine the credibility of the budget and the budget process.

has yet been issued for 1995 by economic classification.

In addition to the impact of "new promises" and the unanticipated cuts they force in other areas, and the effects of expenditure sequestration, many of the important wage decisions are often made after the budget has been approved and are not always consistent with the wage coefficients included in the budget at the time of its preparation. Because of the large weight of wages in total spending (probably

Budget Financing

Treasury bill auctions were started by the Ministry of Finance in May 1993. The authorities' motivation appears to have been twofold: to tap an important source of resources for financing the fiscal deficit and to widen the range of market-based instruments with which the central bank could conduct monetary policy. Given the large deficits registered in the early part of the transition, the recourse to central bank

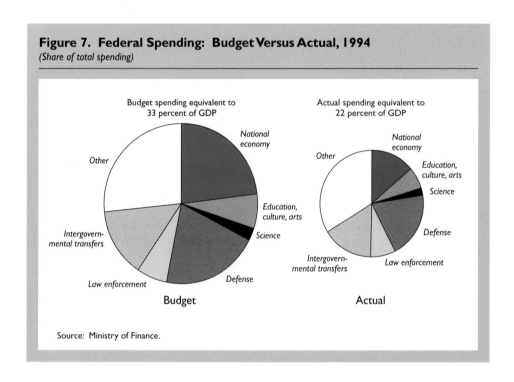

Figure 7. Federal Spending: Budget Versus Actual, 1994
(Share of total spending)

Source: Ministry of Finance.

Table 11. Financing of the Federal Deficit
(In trillions of rubles)

	1992	1993	1994	1995	1996
Financing of the deficit	2.0	11.2	69.7	88.5	186.5
Net foreign financing	–0.1	–0.1	0.1	–3.1	14.5
Domestic financing	2.1	11.3	69.6	91.7	172.0
Banking system	1.9	11.2	61.0	79.6	152.5
Monetary authorities	2.4	11.2	53.5	24.1	48.4
Banking system	–0.5	—	7.5	55.6	104.1
Nonbank	0.2	0.1	8.6	12.1	17.5

Sources: Ministry of Finance; and IMF staff calculations.

credit with the associated repercussions for the price level, and the limited scope for securing additional foreign financing, the authorities felt that treasury bill issues would fill an important void as both instruments of monetary control and public debt management. While, in net terms, financing of the budget that year through issues of treasury bills was small (less than Rub 200 billion, equivalent to 0.1 percent of GDP) and consisted almost exclusively of three-month maturities, gross issues were increased significantly in 1994 and thereafter and began to cover an expanding share of the federal deficit (Table 11). For the 1995 budget the government adopted a two-pronged strategy—while projecting a sharp reduction in the deficit, it moved to eliminate direct central bank credits altogether, theretofore granted at a yearly nominal interest rate of 10 percent.

A move from central bank financing to treasury bill financing, whether through the banking system or the nonbank public or both, transfers the costs of the deficit from one source—the central bank—to another, the budget.[40] Central bank financing in Russia had led to the rapid growth of the monetary base and created a need for extensive sterilization—to stem the inflationary impact—at a time when, other than through interventions in the foreign exchange market, the availability of such instruments was strictly limited. As has been observed in other countries, the high reserve requirements usually associated with sizable sterilization operations (equivalent

to taxation levied through the financial system) tend to lead to a large spread between borrowing and lending rates as banks attempt to preserve profitability through high lending rates on that portion of their assets not subject to reserve requirements, and/or relatively low rates on deposits.[41] In Russia the treasury bill market appeared and then grew in the context of a highly inflationary environment and at a time when confidence in the ability of the government to fulfill its obligations was not high, given certain past developments involving callbacks of banknotes, the blocking of foreign exchange deposits at the Vneshekonombank, and delays in the reimbursement of commodity bonds, all of which had undermined government credibility. These factors, together with widespread perceptions that legal protection of debt holders is quite weak, helped create a situation characterized by relatively short maturities and high nominal and real interest rates. In addition, exchange rate stability during much of 1995–97 turned high ruble real interest rates into high dollar real interest rates as well. Weak budgetary revenues and tight foreign financing thus contributed to growing domestic borrowing and continued upward pressures on interest rates.

Treasury bill financing is not necessarily a particularly severe constraint in the conduct of fiscal pol-

---

[40]The case is sometimes made that in either case the costs are borne by the budget although through different mechanisms. Unremunerated or below-market credit to the government will reduce—or totally eliminate—the transfer of central bank profits, frequently an important source of nontax revenue.

[41]This interest rate wedge has well-known adverse allocational repercussions. It introduces distortionary effects on savings and investment and thus represents a form of taxation of the economy's productive sectors. In the extreme case of unsterilized central bank financing, the result will be inflation, which is also a form of taxation. In Russia during the first half of 1995, the difference between the monthly interbank lending rate and the deposit rate for legal entities amounted to more than 20 percentage points.

icy if the deficits are small or declining with respect to GDP and, furthermore, has none of the negative impact that central bank financing has on the allocation of financial resources. However, if the budget deficit is expected to be relatively high over the medium term and the economy is characterized by high inflation, agents will show a marked preference for short-term instruments and demand an interest rate premium. In conditions of high inflation the fiscal deficit then becomes a function of both the stock of public debt and the level of the nominal interest rate and, through it, the inflation rate. In Russia at the end of 1996 domestic debt was equivalent to about 12 percent of GDP and total debt was around 35 percent of GDP.

Because it is often difficult to reduce current expenditure, the authorities may, in an effort to keep the deficit within agreed levels, find it tempting to reduce public investment expenditure or outlays for human capital, both of which are likely to have adverse implications for future growth. A distortion may then be introduced in the pattern of public investment expenditure as projects are no longer judged on the strength of their merits but rather on the extent to which they might contribute, in the short run, to a widening of the deficit. The sensitivity of the interest component of public expenditure to fluctuations in interest rates may also impose additional constraints on the exercise of monetary policy and may lead to attempts to push interest rates on government paper down merely on the grounds that not to do so would prove a threat to the budget. This higher degree of intervention in the financial markets could come at a time when attempts are being made to move toward freer, less-regulated financial markets. This "forced" reduction of interest rates may in turn result in net reductions in the holdings of treasury bills by the nonbank sector as the relative rates of return on alternative assets go up.[42]

As Russia's financial market is developed and a process of accumulation of interest-bearing government debt in the hands of the nonbank sector deepens,[43] it will be necessary to ensure that an additional source of uncertainty is not introduced in the evolution of the monetary aggregates and, by implication, in the implementation of monetary policy. While in Russia the bulk of treasury bills remain within the banking system—and thus at least in theory subject to whatever reserve requirements the monetary authorities might consider consistent with the achievement of the monetary targets—the emergence of a large market for bills in the hands of the nonbank sector in a context of still relatively high inflation could serve as a potential source of instability for the financial system.

However, if it is assumed that the government will follow over the medium term a reasonably cautious, consistent, and responsible course as regards financial policies—and as part of which there will be no manipulation of interest rates—then these instruments should prove to be an important source of noninflationary finance. Furthermore, the emergence of the treasury bill as an additional policy instrument for the conduct of monetary policy should be regarded as a welcome development. Purchases and sales of government securities in the market to influence liquidity in the system should enhance the central bank's capacities in the area of monetary control.

---

[42]A key issue associated with the question of the desirability of developing a market for public debt is whether the instruments chosen will encourage additional savings or whether they will simply lead to asset substitution. If the intent of the authorities is to encourage savings—while at the same time remaining faithful to a policy of diminishing intervention in the financial system—some form of indexation of treasury bills could be considered. A lengthening of maturities may alleviate pressures on the financial system but will not reduce the burden on the budget.

[43]One-year government obligations (OGSZs) began to be sold to the nonbank public in the fall of 1995. The notes were introduced as bearer obligations carrying four coupons for quarterly interest payments. More recently, two-year obligations carrying four coupons for semiannual interest payments were introduced. As of end-1997 some Rub 13 trillion had been issued in denominations of Rub 100,000 and Rub 500,000. The potential market is seen to be large.

V Social Conditions and Social Protection: Issues and Options

The adjustment experience of transition economies attests to the important effects of macroeconomic policies on income distribution and social equity and welfare. An effective adjustment program must therefore take these effects into account, particularly because they impinge on the most vulnerable or disadvantaged groups in society. This is especially important in a country such as Russia, where the process of transition has brought about serious social dislocations associated with the sharp contraction of output, major shifts in the composition of output, and other systemic factors (see below). In the last several years Russia has also witnessed a severe worsening of the distribution of income. The ratio of the income of the top to the bottom decile rose from 5 in 1991 to 13.5 at the end of 1995, while the Gini coefficient of incomes rose from 0.24 in January 1992 to well over 0.5 in late 1994 (World Bank, 1995b). Income distribution in Russia has become more unequal than in most developed industrial countries and has been accompanied by a pronounced deterioration of living conditions for the poor. These trends are particularly disturbing, since a fairly extensive body of empirical research shows that higher income inequality can contribute to political instability, which in turn depresses private investment and adversely affects future economic growth. Higher income inequality has also been linked to inflationary pressures.[44]

A critical challenge facing Russian economic policy in the years ahead is how to bring about the necessary adjustment and achieve some of the key macroeconomic objectives of the transition to a market economy. These include the establishment of a stable macroeconomic environment, the transfer of certain social functions from the enterprise sector to the state, the rule of law, and continued integration with the world economy, with the least amount of hardship to the most vulnerable social groups and without an aggravation of the income distribution trends mentioned above.[45] Apart from ethical considerations concerning the responsibility of the state in the area of social protection, proper consideration of the impact of economic policy measures on social conditions can produce stronger public support for a particular economic policy and government, making such policies more sustainable.

This section presents an overview of the main policy issues in the area of social protection in Russia. Following a discussion of social conditions, the main elements of the existing social safety net are presented and a number of policy options for improvements are identified.

An Overview of Social Conditions

Income and Consumption Measures

Income and consumption-based welfare indicators try to capture the availability of resources necessary for the satisfaction of human needs.[46] Using a hypothetical poverty line equal to 40 percent of the 1989 average wage, the poverty rate in Russia increased from 6.5 percent in 1989 to over 44 percent in December 1993. Over the same period, the number of people living in extreme poverty rose from 2.5 percent to 20.5 percent, somewhat less than the 27 percent estimated by the Ministry of Labor, using a constant poverty line of 60 rubles per capita in 1989 prices.[47] A World Bank–Goskomstat survey carried

---

[44]See Alesina (1998) for a detailed overview of these issues. The higher measured inequality observed during the last several years needs to be seen against the background of considerable "hidden" inequality under the Soviet regime and the underlying data limitations.

[45]In discussing the role of the state in the postsocialist transition, Kornai highlights the sharp worsening in the distribution of income as one of the most serious problems facing economic policymakers.

[46]The sources for the statistics quoted in the text and shown in Tables 12–14 are the comprehensive reports on social conditions in Central and Eastern Europe published by the United Nations Children's Fund (UNICEF) as well as various socioeconomic indicators compiled by the Goskomstat. See United Nations Children's Fund, International Child Development Centre (1993, 1994, 1995, and 1997).

[47]Extreme poverty is associated with incomes below one-half of the official poverty line.

Table 12. Poverty Line and Incidence of Poverty

	Average Per Capita Income	Average Subsistence Minimum	Population with Income Below Subsistence Minimum (in millions)	In Percent of Total Population
	(In thousands of rubles a month)			
1989[1]		0.054	1.9	1.2
1990[1]		0.061	2.3	1.6
1991[1]		0.154	6.1	4.1
1992[1]	4.0	1.895	35.8	24.1
1993[1]	45.2	20.6	44.2	29.9
1994[1]	206.3	86.6	37.3	25.1
1995[1]	532.9	264.1	42.8	28.9
1996[1]	779.0	369.4	31.9	21.5
1995				
January	312.4	179.5	49.4	33.4
February	347.9	201.4	49.9	33.7
March	410.3	218.9	45.1	30.5
April	446.9	234.2	44.0	29.7
May	487.4	254.3	46.5	31.4
June	538.6	277.4	44.5	30.1
July	550.0	293.4	43.0	29.1
August	580.4	286.1	41.4	28.0
September	613.5	286.2	39.0	26.4
October	648.4	297.8	37.0	25.0
November	685.4	313.2	36.7	24.8
December	781.9	327.3	36.6	24.7
1996				
January	638.2	345.0	37.3	25.2
February	681.9	357.0	35.9	24.3
March	735.7	366.0	34.5	23.3
April	773.8	372.0	33.1	22.4
May	725.8	378.0	34.1	23.0
June	777.7	385.0	32.4	21.9
July	791.0	384.0	30.9	20.9
August	793.3	369.0	29.5	19.9
September	769.6	363.0	29.2	19.7
October	822.6	364.0	28.8	19.5
November	823.6	371.0	29.3	19.8
December	1,000.1	379.0	27.3	18.5

Source: Goskomstat.
[1] Annual average.

out in the second half of 1992 showed especially high rates of poverty for children under 15 (46 percent) and families with three or more children (72 percent). In the first quarter of 1995, some 30 percent of the population (or about 45 million people) were estimated to have income levels below a rather austere minimum subsistence level of some Rub 200,000 ($45) a month; by the end of the year the figures showed some improvement, with 37 million people estimated to have income levels below the minimum subsistence level (Table 12). Regardless of the measure chosen, the number of people living in poverty has increased substantially, even if some allowance is made for the mitigating effects of

intrafamily transfers, the growing of one's own food, and other such factors.

Consistent with the sharp drops in real household income observed in the early part of the transition period, average food expenditure shares in Russia rose from 36.1 percent in 1990 to 47.1 percent in 1992.[48] The economic difficulties associated with

---

[48]The evolution of the food share over time, however, could also be affected by other factors besides income and relative prices, such as the move to a market-based system for the allocation of goods and the associated elimination of food subsidies, the elimination of quantitative restrictions on imports, and, in general, the improved availability of goods.

Table 13. Average Monthly Wages and Pensions
(In current rubles)

	Nominal Wages		Nominal Pensions[1]		Social Minimum[1]		Replacement Rate (in percent)[2]
	Average	Minimum	Average	Minimum	Average	Pensioners	
1987	214	70	80	...	...	...	37.4
1988	233	70	83	...	...	...	35.6
1989	263	70	88	...	...	...	33.4
1990	303	70	102	70	...	...	33.7
1991	548	180	185	151	...	...	33.8
1992	5,995	900	1,500	1,100	1,900	1,300	25.0
1993	58,663	14,620	19,900	11,300	20,600	14,400	33.9
1994	220,351	20,500	78,500	40,700	86,600	61,000	35.6
1995	472,400	60,500	188,100	89,600	264,100	186,200	39.8
1996	806,000	72,700	302,300	116,100	356,100	260,500	37.5
1996							
January	654,800	63,250	246,700	101,000	345,500	243,600	
February	684,400	63,250	274,500	109,000	357,400	252,000	
March	745,000	63,250	275,000	107,000	365,500	257,700	
April	746,500	75,900	275,300	105,000	372,400	262,500	
May	779,800	75,900	318,700	120,000	378,100	266,600	
June	837,200	75,900	318,800	117,000	385,100	271,900	
July	842,800	75,900	319,000	118,000	383,600	270,400	
August	831,000	75,900	319,200	123,000	369,200	260,300	
September	848,100	75,900	319,400	125,000	363,000	256,000	
October	843,300	75,900	319,800	125,000	364,000	256,000	
November	835,000	75,900	320,300	123,000	371,000	261,000	
December	1,017,000	75,900	320,700	120,000	379,000	267,000	

Source: Goskomstat.
[1]Including all benefits and allowances, average pension during last month.
[2]Ratio of average pension to average wage.

the transition have affected both those already living near the poverty line in the pretransition period and consisting mainly of pensioners subsisting on minimum pensions, single-parent families, and families with several children, and others who, while not necessarily near the poverty line at that time, saw their real incomes eroded as a result of the particularly harsh effect of the transition on their individual sectors or industries. An example of the latter might be workers and research scientists living in "closed" cities affiliated with the military-industrial complex in outlying regions of Russia, engineers working in heavy industry, as well as public sector workers employed in education and health centers. The relatively low ratio of the minimum pension to the average wage suggests that pensioners living on the minimum pension have been the most adversely affected group. At the end of 1996, about 7 million pensioners (20 percent of the total) were receiving a minimum pension of $21 a month, well below the minimum subsistence level. Within this group, single pensioners are the most vulnerable subgroup, the majority of whom are women. Also, the ratio of the

average pension to the average wage (the so-called replacement rate) was about 37 percent in 1996, low by international standards (Table 13). The real value of pensions has also fallen, reflecting infrequent discretionary adjustments. In the five-year period to 1996, real minimum pensions fell by some 70 percent and real average pensions fell by 35 percent (Figure 8).

Other Welfare Measures

Income measures of welfare in an economy undergoing profound structural transformations need to be interpreted with care, given the large fluctuations in relative prices, and the shifts in the structure of the economy and in the sources (formal or informal) of activity and income. A fuller picture of social conditions is thus obtained by supplementing income-based indicators with other measures that attempt to capture certain aspects of the quality of life, particularly in the areas of family life, reproductive behavior, mortality, and migration (Table 14). Between 1989 and 1994, these indicators in Russia evolved as

Figure 8. Real Average and Minimum Pension
(1991:Q4 = 100)

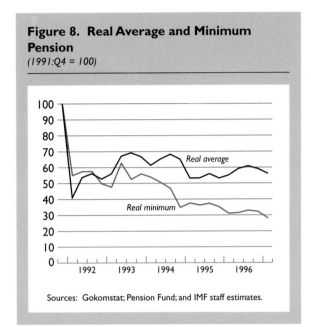

Sources: Gokomstat; Pension Fund; and IMF staff estimates.

follows: (1) a 36 percent drop in the crude birth rate; (2) a 46 percent increase in the crude death rate over the same period, by far the highest rise in the region;[49] (3) a six-year decline in the life expectancy for men, to 58 years, which is below the age of retirement; (4) sharp increases in the incidence of certain diseases (diphtheria, measles, and tuberculosis), sometimes reaching epidemic proportions; and (5) extremely large increases in violent deaths and the incidence of crime in general, including a 137 percent increase in homicides and a 53 percent increase in suicides.[50] A comprehensive set of 29 indicators of welfare, ranging from indicators based on measures of income and consumption to others that attempt to capture the quality of life (mortality, health, and education) show that in Russia, between 1989 and 1994, 27 of these indicators deteriorated, often markedly.

Explanatory Factors

The above profile, which demographers and public health experts have characterized as "alarming" and "without precedent in the European peacetime recent history of this century," reflects a number of interrelated and sometimes mutually reinforcing factors.[51]

First, the sharp deterioration in most indicators of human welfare reveals the presence of an already precarious and extremely vulnerable social environment at the outset of the transition. Unfavorable starting conditions stemming from poorly designed public health policies during the two decades preceding the onset of market reforms left the populations of these countries ill-prepared to withstand the short-term adverse effects of certain measures, such as price liberalization. Some (possibly large) share of the increase in mortality registered in the late 1980s and early part of the 1990s resulted from prolonged periods of environmental neglect and contamination, and lifestyles and nutritional habits inconsistent with healthy living, all compounded by a marked worsening in the quality of health services available to the population at large.[52] Since toxic emissions in the U.S.S.R. were high by international standards, significant parts of the population were exposed to high levels of radiation and, as a result, up to 17 percent of the U.S.S.R. had been declared an ecological crisis area.

Second, the transition itself has brought about fundamental changes in the psychosocial environment, generating what has been called a "social adaptation crisis" (United Nations Children's Fund, International Child Development Centre (1994, p. vi)). The rapid disappearance of traditional institutions and assumptions has left broad segments of the population especially vulnerable to the economic effects of the transition. Social scientists give several reasons: uncertainties about the ability of parents to provide for their families; loss of self-esteem associated with the sense that work experience accumulated during decades of Communism has, overnight, become largely irrelevant in the emerging market place; deep frustration with the drastic erosion in the real value of pensions and the violation of the implicit social contract (that is, that an old-age pension would guarantee a certain dignified standard of living in the future); and, equally important, mental habits and values, coupled with "negative conflict-solving behaviors

---

[49]For those countries for which the data are available in Eastern and Central Europe, the Baltic countries, and several states of the former Soviet Union (a combined total of 18 states), UNICEF calculates a measure of "excess mortality" equal to the absolute number of people who have died in a given period as a result of increases in death rates, netting out the effect of changes in the size and age structure of the population. Excess mortality in Russia during 1990–93 amounted to about 600,000 people, two-thirds of which corresponded to 1993.

[50]These two rates are for the period 1989–93.

[51]United Nations Children's Fund, International Child Development Centre (1994, p. v).

[52]For an eloquent account of the deterioration of health services as it affected the Soviet female population, see Plessix Gray (1989). According to UNICEF, in 1988 one-third of pediatric hospitals had no hot water, 70 percent lacked essential equipment for common medical emergencies and basic drugs, and laboratory materials were generally in short supply. The consumption of animal fat and other cholesterol-rich products in the U.S.S.R. was three times higher than the level recommended by the World Health Organization.

Table 14. Social Conditions

	1985	1990	1991	1992	1993	1994	1995
Birth rate (per 1,000)[1]	16.7	13.4	12.1	10.7	9.4	9.6	9.4
Death rate (per 1,000)	11.3	11.2	11.4	12.2	14.5	15.7	14.8
Marriage rate (per 1,000)	9.7	8.9	8.6	7.1	7.5	7.4	7.2
Fertility rate (children per women)[2]	2.1	1.9	1.7	1.6	1.4	1.4	1.4
Abortion rate (per 1,000 live births)	187.5	206.3	201.0	216.4	235.2	217.3	202.8
Life expectancy at birth (years)							
Men	64.0	63.8	63.5	62.0	58.9	57.6	58.3
Women	74.0	74.3	74.3	73.8	71.9	71.2	71.7
Infant mortality rate (per 1,000 live births)[3]	20.8	17.4	17.8	18.0	19.9	18.6	17.6
Mortality rate of (per 1,000)							
Young adults (aged 20–39)	2.0	2.5	2.7	3.2	4.1	4.5	4.0
Middle-age adults (aged 40–59)	10.4	9.4	9.5	10.7	13,6	15.4	14.5
Elderly adults (aged 60+)	53.4	48.8	48.6	49.9	56.7	60.3	57.0
Secondary enrollment rate (percent of relevant population)	98.9	95.3	93.6	92.3	91.4	91.8	92.0
Total crime rate (per 100,000 population)	989	1,240	1,462	1,857	1,885	1,775	1,858
Homicide rate (per 100,000 (males aged 14–17 years)	—	11.3	11.9	14.1	23.3	29.9	27.4
New cases of tuberculosis	—	50,600	50,400	53,100	63,591	...	...
New cases of diphtheria	—	1,211	1,869	3,897	15,239	...	...

Sources: United Nations Children's Fund, 1993, 1994, 1995, 1997; and Goskomstat.
[1]Number of total births in a year per 1,000 midyear population.
[2]Overall measures of fertility representing the sum of age-specific birth rates over all ages of the child-bearing period.
[3]Annual number of deaths of infants less than age one per 1,000 live births.

which have long prevailed in the region and which include frequent recourse to drinking, violence against family members and, finally, against themselves."[53]

Third, while some increase in poverty rates was inevitable at the outset of price liberalization, the government's failure to bring inflation down to low and stable levels had the predictable effects on per capita income and hence adverse welfare costs on key segments of the population. The absence of political consensus on the ends and means of the economic reform program, particularly in the initial stages of the transition period, also delayed structural reforms and sharply limited the supply response associated with certain measures. At the same time, social safety net issues received inadequate attention, which greatly intensified the plight of vulnerable groups, as well as of those employed in the industrial sector, particularly the military-industrial complex.

Fourth, on the institutional front, the rapid curtailment in the intermediary role of the public sector in the economy, sometimes associated with the privatization process, sometimes linked to the need to bring the public finances under control, accelerated the breakdown of long-established Soviet institutions that had performed a vital social safety net role (such as cultural, sports, and vacation camps; public libraries; and art centers) but did not result in the emergence of adequate substitutes related to organizations of civil society. A general relaxation of health inspections and traffic and labor safety norms, together with rapidly rising crime, contributed to a

[53]United Nations Children's Fund, International Child Development Centre (1994, p. 53).

worsening of some of these indicators. Indeed, this institutional collapse has entailed significant social costs over and above those linked to purely economic factors.

Fifth, severe deficiencies in governance, arising from certain institutional weaknesses, have characterized the transition period. In Russia, in particular, these deficiencies have at times led to situations in which, faced with the need to strengthen the process of macroeconomic stabilization and thus to implement a tight fiscal policy, on a number of occasions government initiatives resulted in the granting of tax exemptions and/or deferrals to certain enterprises and/or lobby groups, with detrimental implications for budgetary revenues. In the context of nominal budget deficits agreed upon at the outset of the fiscal year, these initiatives necessarily led to the compression of expenditures, including in such areas as education, public health, and human capital investment. A strong case can be made that many of the policies implemented in the context of the transition—price and trade liberalization and privatization—were long overdue and, indeed, essential components of the process of modernization of the Russian economy. Hence, some adverse short-term effects were inevitable, particularly given the enormous distortions in resource allocation inherited from the past. Discretionary tax exemptions and privileges, granted on criteria quite removed from efficiency considerations, have made the adjustment process more painful than otherwise would have been the case. The sharp expenditure cuts have affected health services and other welfare expenditures and have led to greater social instability and an erosion of public support for market reforms in general.

Finally, exogenous factors have also played a role. The collapse of the CMEA and, subsequently, the disturbances to trade and financial relations in the context of the dissolution of the Soviet Union, as well as various ethnic and regional conflicts, at times resulting in violent confrontations with losses of human life, have exacerbated the welfare losses associated with the transition. In addition, in Russia, protectionism among partner countries has likewise impeded a faster reorientation of exports.[54]

---

[54]The process of integration of the Russian economy with the rest of the world has at times taken place against a backdrop of significant trade restrictions in foreign markets and the threat of the imposition of new ones. These restrictions have taken the form of antidumping procedures and quantitative restrictions of exports of steel, aluminum, and other commodities. Some of these problems are expected to be ameliorated by membership in the World Trade Organization (WTO), especially in the area of antidumping, where established, reasonably transparent procedures exist and are applied. WTO principles also exist for quantitative restrictions that would mitigate present discriminatory practices.

Social Protection

The most important component of the safety net in Russia, accounting for the bulk of expenditures on social protection, are old-age pensions received by 29.2 million pensioners at the end of 1996, equivalent to nearly 20 percent of the population. An additional 4.1 million people received disability pensions and 2.3 million others received survivors' pensions (also referred to as "loss of breadwinner" pensions). A further 2.0 million people received a variety of other pensions (for example, veterans pensions and "social" pensions to workers with less than five years of employment) bringing the total number of pensioners to 37.6 million, or over one-fourth of the Russian population (Table 15). The retirement age is 60 years for men and 55 for women, although lower ages apply to certain groups. For instance, the retirement age for coal miners and the military is 45 years, and even lower ages may apply in many cases.[55] It is estimated that up to one-fourth of all pensioners have retired under some type of early retirement scheme.

Present legislation allows pensioners who are able and wish to continue to work to receive both pension and salary, with the extra years of service adding on to the value of the pension. Pensions other than for old age typically involve a reduced level of benefit; for instance, disability pensions are capped at the minimum pension, and social pensions, which are funded through the federal budget, are also paid at two-thirds of the minimum pension. It is estimated that about 7 million pensioners received the minimum pension at the end of 1996.[56]

Table 13 shows the recent evolution of the monthly minimum and average pensions, both inclusive of price compensation allowances. At the end of 1996, these stood at Rub 120,000 (about $22) and Rub 321,000 (about $58), respectively. The table also shows the pensioner-specific average subsistence minimum that, at the end of 1996, stood at Rub 267,000, which shows that the minimum pension is less than 50 percent of the already austere average subsistence minimum and that the average pension is equivalent to 85 percent of the average subsistence minimum. By 1996 over 60 percent of all pensioners were receiving pensions that were equivalent to less

---

[55]Other groups that are entitled to early retirement include civil aviation personnel and workers in health and educational institutions, artistic and entertainment establishments, and "jobs characterized by adverse labor conditions".

[56]Official data issued by the Pension Fund show that 3.7 million pensioners receive the minimum pension. However, there are other groups, such as the 2.3 million pensioners on survivors' pensions, for which the benefit does not exceed the minimum level.

Table 15. Population and Pensioners

| | | Pensioners (in millions) | | | | Share of Pensioners in Population (in percent) |
| | | | Of which: | | Population (in millions) | |
	Total	Old age	Disability	Loss of Breadwinner		
1981	27.4	19.5	3.5	3.9	139.6	19.6
1986	30.3	22.5	3.5	3.7	144.8	20.9
1987	30.8	23.2	3.5	3.5	146.0	21.1
1988	31.3	23.8	3.5	3.3	147.0	21.3
1989	31.7	24.6	3.5	2.9	147.7	21.5
1990	32.2	25.2	3.6	2.6	148.2	21.7
1991	32.8	25.7	3.5	2.8	148.3	22.1
1992	34.0	27.1	3.4	2.6	148.3	22.9
1993	35.3	28.4	3.4	2.5	148.0	23.9
1994	36.1	29.0	3.6	2.4	147.9	24.4
1995	36.6	29.1	3.9	2.4	147.6	24.8
1996	37.6	29.2	4.1	2.3	147.9	25.4

Source: Pension Fund.

than three minimum pensions, that is, somewhat below the minimum subsistence level for the general population. Virtually all others received pensions that ranged between 3 and 3.5 minimum pensions. Given the compression of pensions and the level of the average subsistence minimum, the bulk of pensioners have incomes at or below the poverty line. This is also reflected in the consumption patterns of pensioners: 75 percent of pensioners' income is spent on food, and the diet is heavily slanted toward basic staples (bread, potatoes, vegetable oil, and so on); pensioners have had growing difficulties in meeting other basic expenses, such as for public utilities, and have had to postpone indefinitely others, such as the purchase of some consumer durables. Given this difficult situation and despite the absence of systematic data, it appears that many pensioners have been forced to earn additional income by remaining at their place of employment. Some surveys suggest that, at least in the larger urban centers, up to 20 percent of pensioners have continued to work past the retirement age and, hence, in the case of male workers, past the average life expectancy. The Pension Fund estimates that approximately 8 million pensioners—21.5 percent of the total number of beneficiaries—continue to work beyond the retirement age.

Because of infrequent adjustments to changes in the cost of living, average and minimum pensions in real terms have fallen precipitously during the past several years. By 1996 they stood at 65 percent and 30 percent,

respectively, of their 1991 levels.[57] The average pension on December 1995 was a full 14 percent lower in real terms than the same pension a year earlier, and the real drop in the minimum pension over the same period was 21 percent. Pensions were increased in February and May 1996, and by the end of 1996, the minimum pension stood at some 80 percent of the minimum subsistence level, although, as of end-1997, there was no formal linkage between the minimum pension and the minimum subsistence level (see below).

Pensions are financed through the Pension Fund, the bulk of its resources generated from payroll contributions. Employer contributions to the Pension Fund are assessed at 28 percent of gross pay, although the rate for agricultural enterprises and the self-employed are lower, at 20.6 and 5 percent, respectively. Employee contributions are set at 1 percent. Because of exemptions and arrears in payments of contributions—which exceeded 2 percent of GDP at the end of 1996—the effective contribution rate for the general scheme is well below the statutory rate of 29 percent (see below).[58]

---

[57]For instance, between November 1, 1994 and May 1, 1995, prices, as measured by the consumer price index, grew by a cumulative 106 percent; the minimum pension (including price compensation allowances) was increased by 54 percent. The average pension rose by 72 percent over the same period.

[58]Approximately 93 percent of all revenue collected by the Pension Fund is derived from the general scheme, for which the employer contribution rate is 28 percent. Agricultural workers account for some 5 percent and the remaining 2 percent of revenue corresponds to the self-employed.

In addition to pensions, a number of other benefits are provided through various extrabudgetary funds (Figure 9). The Social Insurance Fund (SIF) provides sick, maternity, and birth allowances and a broad range of other benefits. It finances these benefits from employer contributions assessed at 5.4 percent of gross pay collected on some 61 million workers (Table 16). The bulk of these resources (approximately 85 percent on average) are administered by the enterprises themselves, with the remaining share going to the SIF to cover administrative expenditures and the payment of benefits to other recipients. As presently administered, enterprises collect the contributions and pay the benefits dictated by the law; leftover amounts are remitted to the SIF, which may have to finance "deficit" enterprises and/or regions.[59] Sick pay is provided at 100 percent of pay for employees with eight or more years of service, to large families (at least three children) and to certain special groups, such as Chernobyl victims, war veterans, and Northern Territories residents. The benefit is reduced to 80 percent of pay for length of service between five and eight years and to 60 percent for less than five years. Sick pay is, in principle, available "until recovery," or until the employee is judged to be eligible to receive an invalidity pension.

In 1996, the average number of sick days paid per worker was 8.3; it was 14 for those actually ill. Sick pay is also available when caring for a family member, although certain time limits may apply (for example, 14 days a year for the care of a child over 14 years of age). For younger children (less than 14 years of age) and for single mothers (regardless of the age of the child), however, there is no limit, which may explain the relatively large share in total sick pay outlays of this particular benefit (15 percent). In addition, the SIF subsidizes the expenses of a large number of sanatoriums attached to enterprises; these subsidies typically take the form of payments for utilities, food, and medical personnel. Subsidies are also provided for vacations (implicit subsidy of 90 percent, but limited to a small fraction of beneficiaries[60]) and children's summer camps. These expenditures account for nearly 23 percent of total SIF expenditures. As with the Pension Fund, arrears have accumulated in employer contributions to the SIF. On October 1, 1996, these stood at Rub 5 trillion, equivalent to nearly 20 percent of total expenditures. The counterpart of this has been a "squeeze" in the level of some of the benefits and growing delays in their payment, although no figures are available on the extent of this phenomenon.

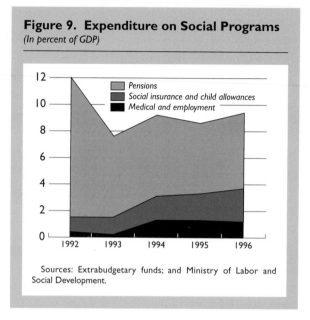

Figure 9. Expenditure on Social Programs
(In percent of GDP)

Sources: Extrabudgetary funds; and Ministry of Labor and Social Development.

Until May 1995, the maternity grant consisted of a single payment equivalent to five minimum wages; it was then raised to 10 minimum wages and, on January 1, 1996, it was set at 15 minimum wages; this benefit is made available regardless of whether the mother is employed or not. Mothers also receive a birth allowance set at 100 percent of their wage, irrespective of length of service, payable for a period of 140 to 180 days; subsequently, a benefit equal to two minimum wages is provided for an additional 18 months.[61]

Children's allowances are provided to all families, irrespective of the level of income. Children up to the age of 16 receive a benefit equal to 70–140 percent of the minimum wage, although the benefit rises if the mother is single; if either parent serves in the army, the security forces, or a number of other public institutions (such as the Ministry of Foreign Affairs); or if the child is due alimony payments and these are not received. The benefit is also payable to children up to the age of 18 if they are full-time school students.[62]

In Russia, 34.8 million children are officially eligible to receive the allowance. Although no figures are available on the number of actual recipients, the Ministry of Labor and Social Development estimates that, at the end of 1995, about 80 percent of those eligible actually applied and received the allowance. It is not clear why so many others did not apply although it is presumed that several factors played a role. These in-

---

[59]In the textile sector, for instance, payment of benefits significantly exceeds revenues from contributions. The SIF then is required to step in and provide the difference.

[60]About 630,000 vouchers were issued in 1995.

[61]This benefit was equal to one minimum wage until the end of 1995.

[62]Until May 1995 the benefit was payable at 70 percent of the minimum wage only if the child was less than 6 years old; the benefit was reduced to 60 percent for ages between 6 and 16 years.

Table 16. Social Insurance Fund
(In trillions of rubles)

	1993	1994	1995	1996
Revenues	2.11	7.87	18.80	28.80
Of which:				
Contributions	1.87	6.89	15.98	25.69
Expenditures	1.74	6.66	16.66	28.14
Of which:				
Sick pay	0.87	3.69	8.90	14.33
Maternity allowance[1]	0.13	0.49	1.02	1.80
Maternity grant	0.02	0.10	0.37	1.57
Maternity leave[2]	0.06	0.25	0.61	2.48
Sanatoriums and health-related	0.34	1.50	3.73	4.68
Children's summer camps	0.06	0.22	1.17	1.54
Administrative expenditures	0.04	0.24	0.53	1.13
Memorandum items:				
Benefit recipients (in millions)	63.5	62.6	61.2	60.8
Average number of sick days/employee	8.6	8.1	8.4	8.3
Recipients of maternity grant (in millions)	1.3	1.2	1.2	1.2
Number of authorized stays at health facilities (in millions)	9.8	7.9	9.1	7.4
Of which:				
Treatment and healing	3.7	2.8	2.9	2.1
Children's summer camps	3.1	3.3	4.7	4.2

Source: Social Insurance Fund.
[1]Before and after childbirth, payable at 100 percent of pay for 140 to 180 days.
[2]Payable at two minimum wages a month for an additional 18 months.

clude the relatively small size of the allowance (which averaged $9 a month during 1995), arbitrary interpretation of implementing guidelines at the oblast level with officials refusing payment to otherwise eligible recipients (for example, workers in the "informal" sector), and lack of information on eligibility requirements in general. Much of the financing is provided through the regional budgets, although part of the federal transfers allocated to the regions are also intended to finance children's allowances. In addition, all children's allowances for defense and security personnel are paid out of federal funds. Approximately one-third of all oblasts—mainly those located in the Northern Territories—receive the allowances adjusted by a "regional coefficient," which ranges from 1.1 to 2.6 times the regular allowance. Total expenditures on children's allowances amounted to Rub 4.5 trillion in

1994 (0.7 percent of GDP), Rub 14 trillion in 1995 (0.9 percent of GDP), and are estimated to have reached Rub 31 trillion, or 1.4 percent of GDP in 1996 (Table 17). On June 1, 1996, arrears on the payment of children's allowances amounted to Rub 3 trillion, Rub 700 billion of which corresponded to 1995 allowances.

The rate of unemployment in Russia stood at 9.3 percent of the labor force in December 1996, affecting 6.8 million people (Table 18). The number of registered unemployed that month was 2.5 million, an 8 percent increase compared with a year earlier and a nearly fivefold increase compared with the same period in 1992. Unemployment benefits are provided through the Employment Fund, which receives payroll contributions from employers equivalent to 1.5 percent of gross pay.[63] These resources are shared on a 20:80 basis between the federal and regional (oblast) employment funds. The regional share in turn is further distributed between regional and local funds although there is no fixed formula for this, with the distribution left to the discretion of the regional authorities. Of the 89 regions in Russia, 47 received in 1996 some form of transfer from the federal share, to compensate for insufficiency of resources after the payment of benefits at the regional level.

First-time job seekers receive a benefit equal to the minimum wage. Unemployed workers with prior job experience receive, during a 4-month period, 75 percent of their average monthly wage during the preceding 3-month period prior to loss of their jobs; the benefit is reduced to 60 percent during the following 4 months and 45 percent for the next 4 months. Beyond the first year the worker may receive a benefit equivalent to one minimum monthly wage for a 6-month period but needs to reapply for the benefit on a monthly basis. After this initial 18-month period, and following a 6-month period in which he or she is not eligible to receive unemployment compensation, the worker may reapply and receive one minimum monthly wage during an additional 12-month period and may also supplement this income with stipends for participation in public works projects. Unemployment benefits accounted for 29 percent of total Employment Fund expenditure in 1995, up from 18 percent in 1994.

The Employment Fund also allocates resources to training, early pensions,[64] and financial support to

---

[63]The contribution rate was reduced from 2 percent to 1.5 percent on January 1, 1996. The Employment Fund estimates the adverse impact on revenues in 1996 to be some Rub 2.5–3 trillion.

[64]Some 130,000 workers have used this option, retiring a full two years before the age of retirement. The Employment Fund transfers to the Pension Fund the resources needed to finance this.

Table 17. Expenditure on Social Programs

	1992	1993	1994	1995	1996
	(In trillions of rubles)				
Pension Fund	1.9	10.4	37.4	86.3	129.0
Social Insurance Fund	0.2	1.6	6.7	17.6	25.4
Children's allowances[1]	—	0.7	4.5	14.0	31.0
Medical Fund	—	—	5.7	14.2	20.4
Employment Fund	0.1	0.4	2.4	6.4	6.9
Total	2.6	13.1	56.7	138.5	212.7
	(In percent of GDP)				
Pensions	10.5	6.1	6.1	5.3	5.7
Social Insurance Fund	1.1	0.9	1.1	1.1	1.1
Children's allowances[1]	—	0.4	0.7	0.9	1.4
Medical Fund	—	—	0.9	0.9	0.9
Employment Fund	0.4	0.2	0.4	0.4	0.3
Total	12.0	7.6	9.3	8.5	9.4

Sources: Extrabudgetary funds; and Ministry of Labor and Social Development.

[1]Administered by the Ministry of Labor and Social Development.

enterprises "for the protection of existing jobs and the creation of new ones," the latter under two schemes that make resources available to enterprises either in the form of grants or subsidized loans at one-half of the central bank refinance rate, both mainly aimed at vulnerable groups, such as youth, invalids, women with several children, and the long-term unemployed. As with other social funds, arrears in contributions have emerged recently; at the end of 1996, these stood at Rub 3.2 trillion, equivalent to over 100 percent of total unemployment benefits paid out. Arrears in the payment of unemployment benefits were Rub 1.2 trillion. The ratio of the average unemployment benefit to the average wage in 1995 was 20 percent. The sharp increase in under-employment in the form of unpaid leave and shorter working hours, affecting nearly 6 million people at the end of 1996 (about 8 percent of the total labor force), is another characteristic of the labor environment.

Like the other social funds, the Medical Fund, founded in 1993, is financed through employer contributions assessed at 3.6 percent of gross pay, 3.4 percent of which is retained at the regional level and administered by the local offices of the Medical Fund; the remaining share of 0.2 percent is allocated to the center. Contributions accounted for slightly more than 60 percent of total revenues in 1995, with the rest mainly from budgetary transfers at the regional level, to finance services to the unemployed. The Medical Fund provides medical assistance in the form of hospitalizations, emergency assistance, and medicines for in-patient treatment. During 1995,

it handled 16.5 million individual hospitalizations, for an average of 14 days each. The payment of salaries for medical personnel and medicines accounted for 52 percent of the Rub 13.4 trillion spent in 1995 (0.8 percent of GDP). The creation of the Medical Fund is thought to have protected a minimum level of resources for medical assistance from the rigors of expenditure sequestration at the federal level.

Consumer subsidies were an important (and inefficient) source of social protection in Russia during the early part of the transition, particularly in 1992 and 1993, and consisted of commodity subsidies provided through a variety of mechanisms, including the noncollection of counterpart funds associated with the use of tied external credits. While the extent of this form of subsidization through the federal budget has been sharply reduced in recent years, consumer subsidies continue to be provided through local budgets on an ad hoc basis; no reliable figures are available, however. In addition, housing subsidies, mainly subsidies for communal services, may account for as much as 3–4 percentage points of GDP, mostly at the local level.

Policy Issues and Options

Although the creation of the Pension Fund, the Social Insurance Fund, the Employment Fund, and the Medical Fund during 1991–93 was an important step in the establishment of a contribution-based social insurance system, no major changes, other than the in-

Table 18. Unemployment and Vacancies
(In thousands)

	Registered Vacancies	Registered Job Seekers	Registered Unemployment Total	Of which: Receiving benefits	According to International Labor Organization Definition
End-year 1992	315	982	577	371	. . .
End-year 1993	352	1,085	836	550	. . .
End-year 1994	327	1,879	1,637	1,394	5,300
End-year 1995	318	2,549	2,327	2,026	6,000
End-year 1996	260	2,751	2,506	2,259	6,800
1995					
January	311	1,963	1,711	1,457	5,516
February	316	2,096	1,839	1,577	5,670
March	329	2,166	1,921	1,654	5,630
April	368	2,220	1,986	1,709	5,660
May	405	2,226	1,993	1,720	5,682
June	445	2,242	2,004	1,727	5,700
July	454	2,282	2,048	1,764	5,700
August	460	2,335	2,098	1,818	5,700
September	446	2,345	2,104	1,821	5,800
October	404	2,399	2,142	1,854	5,900
November	352	2,491	2,228	1,932	5,900
December	318	2,549	2,327	2,026	6,000
1996					
January	294	2,702	2,418	2,099	6,446
February	287	2,873	2,568	2,230	6,464
March	287	2,974	2,676	2,337	6,476
April	309	3,064	2,771	2,427	6,547
May	327	2,970	2,694	2,372	6,606
June	346	2,867	2,605	2,356	6,665
July	350	2,817	2,558	2,319	6,732
August	343	2,778	2,525	2,302	6,680
September	333	2,725	2,470	2,247	6,700
October	341	2,724	2,451	2,224	6,700
November	274	2,742	2,460	2,226	6,800
December	260	2,751	2,506	2,259	6,800
Memorandum items:		*(In percent of labor force)*			
End-year 1992	0.4	1.3	0.8	0.5	. . .
End-year 1993	0.5	1.5	1.1	0.7	. . .
End-year 1994	0.4	2.5	2.2	1.9	7.5
End-year 1995	0.4	3.5	3.2	2.8	8.3
End-year 1996	0.4	3.8	3.5	3.1	9.3

Source: Goskomstat.

troduction of the unemployment benefit, have taken place in the main *principles* underlying the administration of social protection in Russia. In particular, many benefits continue to be granted universally (that is, not means-tested) and the eligibility criteria for many of these have not been revised to take account of radical changes in the structure of the economy and the needs of various groups within the population. It is important in any discussion of the options available over the medium term to policymakers in the area of social protection to distinguish between the level and the coverage of existing benefits. A key goal of any reform effort should undoubtedly be to protect the most vulnerable groups in society—the old, the unemployed, large or single-parent families, and the disabled. The aim should be to ameliorate the difficult conditions that have emerged in recent years, as evidenced by the income-based and social and demographic indicators discussed earlier. The inevitable resource constraints that the country faces implies that available resources have to be used more effectively; it does not imply that existing levels of social protection are adequate or desirable. To the detriment of the people the system is intended to help, the demands of financial stabilization have often been used in the past as an excuse not to introduce reforms in the existing system of benefits, thus perpetuating a number of rigidities and inefficiencies. As part of any reform effort the possibility has to be admitted that the "right" level of social protection in Russia could involve more spending in specified areas and the curtailment or withdrawal of other benefits to certain groups. Some priorities and possible reforms are discussed below.

(1) Subject to the constraints imposed by the need for fiscal sustainability, the highest priority should be given to moving to a pension system that links in a predictable and reliable way the value of pensions received by Russia's 37 million pensioners to increases in the cost of living. The improvisations of the past several years have not only worked to the detriment of pensioners but have greatly undermined support for the economic reform process. There appear to be no underlying principles in this area. In 1993–96 the authorities increased the minimum pension a number of times; introduced a system of indexation of pensions in 1993; abandoned the system shortly thereafter and replaced it with one that provides a separate flat "price compensation" allowance, itself adjusted in an ad hoc manner not fully reflecting changes in the price level; and raised the overall level of pensions upward through presidential decree (for example, by 51 percent on October 1, 1994). The net result has been, as noted earlier, a drop in the average real value of pensions, growing delays in their payment (equivalent to close to 1 percent of GDP at end-1996), the narrowing of the distribution of pensions, and the concomitant weakening of the link between individual contributions paid and the level of pension received, which has had the effect of moving the pension system closer to a flat pension rather than an earnings-based scheme, with most pensions being pushed to the minimum subsistence level or below.[65] Short of full price indexation, an intermediate step might be to

adjust nominal pensions so as to achieve a given replacement ratio; that is, to establish the average pension at a fraction of the average wage.

(2) One component of the above reform would be an upward adjustment in the level of the minimum pension to the minimum subsistence level and the maintenance of this level through indexation. It is inconsistent and socially costly for a social security system to exist, in which several million pensioners receive a pension that is significantly below a figure that the government itself regards as being the minimum essential for survival.[66] Even the minimum subsistence level, when it was introduced in 1992, was a temporary concept to protect recipients at times of severe crisis. As such it was designed in a way that allocated an overwhelmingly large share to food products and made little (if any) allowance for many other items in the consumption basket. To the extent that there have been substantial increases in the relative prices of items previously assigned a small share in the minimum basket (such as public utilities, which were significantly underpriced in 1992), even the minimum subsistence amount may no longer be adequate to meet basic needs. The perception that the true social conditions of some of these groups may not be as harsh as suggested by the official statistics because a growing share of the population derives income from the "cash economy" does not undermine the desirability of this measure. The fact that because of need many elderly receiving the minimum pension have been driven to find alternative sources of income in order to survive should not be an excuse for not providing them with at least the minimum subsistence income. At the same time, efforts should be made to bring into the tax base alternative sources of income, including for pensioners. It is estimated that the cost of raising the minimum pension to the minimum subsistence level in 1995 would have amounted to some 0.4–0.5 percent of GDP. This measure can also be seen as an effective way to reduce the incidence of poverty among the elderly. A step in this direction was taken in 1997 with the issuance of a presidential decree which calls for the setting of the minimum old-age pension (inclusive of compensations) at 80 percent of the minimum subsistence level, beginning in January 1998.[67]

(3) The Pension Fund's revenue base could be enhanced through a number of measures.

First, there is a need to include in the wage base various in-kind benefits that are provided by enter-

[65]With the aim of establishing, over the medium term, a closer linkage between the magnitude of pensions and the level of individual contributions, the government adopted a resolution in 1997 to establish an Individual Data Center under the jurisdiction of the Pension Fund. (Government Resolution No. 318, dated March 15, 1997, "On Measures to Organize the Registration of Individual State Pensions.")

[66]In 1996 the minimum pension was equivalent to 33 percent of the average minimum subsistence level, well below the corresponding ratio for 1993 (55 percent).

[67]As noted in Decree No. 573, dated June 14, 1997, "On Measures to Maintain the Financial Condition of Pensioners."

prises to their employees and that are tax exempt and thus reduce the definition of gross pay on which contributions are assessed. Some progress began to be made in this area in 1996, but the scope for further progress is ample.

Second, measures need to be taken to narrow the large gap between the statutory contribution rate of 29 percent and an effective rate closer to 20 percent. This can be done by eliminating a number of exemptions, such as the one that allows enterprises in which more than 50 percent of the labor force is classified as "disabled" not to contribute to the Pension Fund, even for the nondisabled workers employed by the enterprise. More generally, it is necessary to phase out many of the preferential early retirement schemes for selected groups of workers that have come to account for a large share of the total pensioner population, have introduced a degree of inequity in Russia's social security system, and have significantly undermined the Pension Fund's revenue base. The urgency of these measures is underscored by estimates made by the Ministry of Labor and Social Development that show fiscal sustainability in the present pension system over the medium term only through a gradual rise in the retirement age (to as much as 65–70 years in the long term) and the elimination of all existing exemptions.[68] The existence of separate regimes for which different contribution rates apply is likewise thought to have led to abuse; for instance, through attempts on the part of enterprises to register or reclassify as "agricultural" and thus benefit from the lower rate. More important, the effective contribution rate has fallen because arrears in employer contributions have been allowed to grow. From some Rub 7 trillion on January 1, 1995, these had reached Rub 83 trillion by the end of 1997 (equivalent to over 3 percentage points of GDP)—a several-fold increase in real terms and spread over virtually every sector of the economy (including the oil and gas sector).

Third, while there is no scope for a further rise in the employers' statutory rate of contribution, which in the case of the Pension, Social Insurance, Medical, and Employment Funds amount to a combined 38.5 percent, the same is not the case with the employees' contribution rate, which stands at 1 percent of gross pay. The disincentive effects associated with a high rate of employers' contribution are well

known and have led to evasion and the rapid growth of the underground economy, with the concomitant adverse effects on the collection of other taxes. It should be possible to move to a system that more equitably distributes the burden of financing between employer and employee without adversely affecting the Pension Fund's revenue base; indeed, this shift could be obtained through an increase in the employee's contribution rate. It is estimated that a 1 percent rise in the contribution rate in 1996 could have resulted in a Rub 4–5 trillion increase in social security revenues.[69]

Fourth, there is also scope to reduce pension benefits to full-time workers who cannot be regarded as being "vulnerable" as a group. Given the wide gap between the average pension and the average wage, it should be possible to limit somewhat the pension benefit to those workers drawing full pay.[70]

(4) Because of sharp regional differences in the extent of price liberalization, with many local governments still providing important subsidies for housing, public transport, utilities, and some essential commodities, there are sharp differences in the cost of living faced by pensioners across the country. These differences are not adequately reflected, however, in the level of pensions across regions. The minimum pension is the same everywhere in Russia. The calculation of other pensions does incorporate certain regional coefficients, but these are largely based on "structural" characteristics (for example, pensioners living in areas affected by the Chernobyl disaster and pensioners unjustly sent to labor camps or who are victims of "repression" would receive a higher pension) rather than differences in the cost of living. In any event, even with these adjustments, the differentiation in the level of pensions (other things being equal) seldom exceeds 10 percent. But differences in the cost of living are much larger. In the interests of equity, the level of pensions should be harmonized to the regional cost of living.

---

[68]There appears to be little support in Russia for increasing the retirement age—which is low by international standards—above 60 years for males. The precipitous decline in the average life expectancy (which has fallen below the retirement age) creates a difficult "perception" problem for those who argue that this measure is necessary to strengthen the revenue base of the Pension Fund. Since the average life expectancy of females is, however, considerably higher, there would appear to be some scope for savings by increasing the retirement age for women, which at present is five years lower than that for males.

[69]The case of Spain is illustrative. At 29.15 percent, employers' contributions in Spain were among the highest in member countries of the Organization for Economic Cooperation and Development in 1980. These were reduced to 24 percent by 1985 while only marginally reducing employees' contribution rates from 5.15 percent to 4.80 percent. A new law on pensions introduced in 1985 significantly tightened eligibility requirements by increasing the length of period required to qualify for a pension and by broadening the coverage of the income on which contributions were paid. Tighter control also contributed to reducing the rate of growth of disability pensions. These measures more than offset the adverse impact of the reduction in contribution rates.

[70]In late 1997 the government adopted a medium-term framework for pension reform that envisages, beginning in 2000, that pensions would be funded through a combination of the present pay-as-you-go system and a capitalized system of individual accounts.

(5) The present division of responsibilities between the Pension Fund and the Ministry of Labor and Social Development leads to severe inefficiencies in administration. The Pension Fund is responsible for the collection of contributions, the setting of fines, and all relations with the federal authorities as regards possible financial transfers from the budget. The Ministry of Labor and Social Development, on the other hand, is in charge of assessing entitlements, calculating benefit levels in light of existing legislation (such as when an adjustment in the minimum wage triggers changes in the level of several benefits), as well as the actual paying of pensions. This creates a situation in which the Pension Fund is effectively "presented with bills" by an agency that has no responsibility for collecting the necessary revenue. This division of functions makes effective management of resources virtually impossible and has already resulted in a number of problems, such as delays in the determination of benefits and the payment of pensions. Delays in the payment of pensions in early 1996 averaged two months, although there were many for whom the delay was much greater. Also reflecting this, there have been large expenditures on overhead (for example, Rub 2.2 trillion for postal charges during 1995, equivalent to some 25 million minimum monthly pensions).

The lack of clarity concerning jurisdiction over their operations also undermines effective management of the various funds. Formally, the funds report to parliament but a 1993 presidential decree assigned some responsibilities to the government. As a result, the funds are not fully accountable to either body, which helps explain the underlying lack of guiding principles.

(6) The fact that the four main social security funds independently collect their own contributions is a burden on the authorities and greatly limits their flexibility. Not only are the collection functions duplicated, with the concomitant increase in administrative costs, but more important, to the extent that the resources generated cannot be transferred from one fund to another (say, from the Social Insurance Fund to the Pension Fund to pay for higher minimum pensions), it introduces a rigidity in the system that sharply limits the authorities' ability to respond to the most urgent needs. It also creates a situation in which some benefits are inadequate in magnitude (such as the minimum pension), while others are not only potentially large but misdirected (such as children's allowances to high-income families with several children; see below). The interests of social protection in Russia would be served well by consolidating these funds into one fund and by giving that fund (for example, the Pension Fund) sole responsibility for collecting and distributing pensions, as well as for administering other benefits.

The costs associated with this segmented approach to the administration of social benefits in Russia cannot be overestimated. For instance, until 1995, the bulk of Employment Fund expenditures were administrative, with less than 20 percent of resources in 1994 actually allocated to unemployment compensation. The apparent reason was the need to develop infrastructure at the Employment Fund for the administration of benefits (computer centers, office space, and so on). Such infrastructure was also being developed at the same time at the other funds, thus creating considerable overlap. This was unfortunate, given the significant needs in the social area in Russia during this period.

Another aspect of the decentralization of benefits administration detracts from more efficient management of scarce resources. At present, the range of benefits offered by each fund are determined by the relative magnitude of the employers' contributions allocated to that particular fund, which in turn have been established at levels necessary to maintain many of the same benefits that existed in Russia in the pretransition period. This has resulted in a distribution of resources across different benefits that no longer reflects the rapidly changing needs of the population several years into the transition and that often involves considerable overlap. By way of illustration, Table 19 shows resources spent in 1995 in unemployment compensation, sick pay, treatment at sanatoriums, in-patient medical care, children's allowances, and minimum pensions. Several observations are warranted: (i) although the unemployment rate has increased sharply in recent years, less than 2 percent of total social expenditure in 1995 went to the payment of unemployment compensation, which remains quite low in relation to the level of wages; (ii) benefits for treatments at sanatoriums through the SIF may duplicate those made available through the Medical Fund and exceed by a factor of 2 those made for unemployment compensation; (iii) children's allowances remain, except for old-age pensions, the single most costly benefit, exceeding by several orders of magnitude outlays on minimum pensions and unemployment compensation.

A key priority of social protection in Russia over the medium term should be to reassess the relative weight that should be attached to each of these benefits within the overall budget for social protection in a way that emphasizes the quality and quantity of services received by the most vulnerable groups in the population rather than maintaining a broad constellation of benefits, often of a universal nature, that reflects pretransition social priorities and conditions. The aim should be to increase the flexibility of the authorities in the administration of scarce resources in a way that gives the highest priority to the interests of the most needy groups.

Table 19. Selected Benefits
(In trillions of rubles)

	1995	In Percent of Total Expenditure	In Percent of GDP
Unemployment compensation	1.9	1.5	0.1
Sick pay	8.9	7.0	0.5
Sanatoriums	3.7	2.9	0.2
In-patient medical care	13.3	10.5	0.8
Children's allowances	14.0	11.1	0.9
Minimum pensions[1]	3.2	2.5	0.2
Total	45.0	35.5	2.8
Memorandum item:			
Total social expenditure[2]	126.6		

Sources: Extrabudgetary funds; and IMF staff estimates.
[1]As defined by Pension Fund.
[2]Including administrative expenditures.

(7) As with pensions, the administration of children's allowances could be improved. First, it is desirable to change its universal nature whereby cash benefits are given to recipients independent of the level of income, a characteristic that introduces inequity in the administration of the allowance, reduces the potential benefits to truly needy families, and significantly adds to total costs. The Ministry of Labor and Social Development estimates that, for instance, if the allowance was made available only to families with two or more children, the yearly savings would amount to some ½ of 1 percent of GDP, funds that could be used to increase the value of the benefit to families, with lower incomes or, in the context of an integrated system of social benefits as discussed above, allocated to other worthy social goals. Second, efforts should be made to reach those needy families, which, for reasons that are not completely clear, are presently not receiving the allowance, particularly in light of some evidence of apparent arbitrariness (or mismanagement) in the administration of the benefit at the oblast level. Third, as with other social benefits in Russia, it is necessary to introduce more regional differentiation in the value of the benefit, given sharp differences in the local cost of living. The present regional coefficients are not an adequate substitute and only partly (and sometimes arbitrarily) compensate families for such differences.

Finally, and perhaps most important, the value of the benefit should be delinked from the level of the minimum wage. Whatever the initial motivations may have been to establish such a linkage, the system has quickly given rise to a situation where decisions to increase the minimum wage are determined by the likely financial implications of the corresponding automatic adjustments to social benefits. A more efficient way to proceed might be to link the value of the benefit to some fixed percentage of the minimum subsistence level and to adjust the latter fully to changes in the cost of living. While officials at the Ministry of Labor and Social Development recognize that there is significant scope for improving the efficiency of resources allocated to the payment of children's allowances, there is also a sense that at present the administrative capacity is not yet in place that would allow the linking of this benefit to some measure of family income.

(8) Much has been written on the need to harden the enterprise budget constraint to address the grievous inefficiencies of the past and because the behavioral patterns implied by the assumptions underlying the existence of a soft budget constraint are inconsistent with the development of a market economy. While the condition of enterprises varies greatly across sectors and regions in Russia, with some having been privatized and thus no longer posing a direct burden on the budget, others have gone or are going through a process of disinvestment and retrenchment. Clearly the ongoing process of restructuring of production by sectors will continue to involve retrenchment in the activities of previously unprofitable enterprises. In addition, it will continue to be necessary to better adapt the size of firms to the needs of a competitive market and to improve productivity. All of these processes have led and will continue to lead to the elimination of jobs and the corresponding rise in unemployment. In such a context, the effective operation of an adequate system of unemployment insurance and compensation assumes a prominent place among macroeconomic policy objectives.

(9) While a strong case can be made for the consolidation of the various social funds into a single one, there is concern that consolidation of these funds into the budget might make their resources vulnerable to the uncertainties of expenditure sequestration. Social spending in general and spending on key elements of the social safety net in particular would then become part of the general expenditure priorities of the government and thus subject to some of the inefficiencies and arbitrariness mentioned earlier. It might therefore be best to move to a system with a single institution in charge of the provision of social benefits, but its resources should be protected from the demands made on the government budget.[71]

---

[71]The potential risks associated with this "confiscation" of resources meant for social expenditure cannot be overestimated. In 1996 the Employment Fund was instructed to transfer Rub 350 billion to the Pension Fund (not necessarily a harmful thing) and Rub 700 billion to the Ministry of Defense for military conversion purposes. Some limited transfers between funds, notably from the SIF to the Pension Fund, in the form of loans were made in 1996.

VI   The Tasks Ahead

Russia has made remarkable progress during the 1990s in laying out the foundations of a market economy and in defining the role of the state within it, both in its capacity as intermediator of a large share of resources and as the primary agent for the establishment of the institutions and rules that govern economic relationships. It is beyond the scope of this chapter to make a listing of the many enduring changes that have characterized this period and that have taken the Russian economy from the days of the Soviet plans, when the state "sought to control all activity in society,"[72] to the first days of economic liberalization, when initial tentative steps were taken aimed at creating the basic elements of a functioning market economy, to the present when the bulk of economic activity is generated within an expanding private sector and in the context of a system of flexible prices reflecting relative scarcities in the marketplace.

Some of the positive developments underlying this process of change have taken place in those areas most closely linked with the fiscal functions of the government and have involved, for instance, moves toward the establishment of a tax system freer of some of the distortions of the past, which has enhanced the transparency and efficiency of existing taxes and is closer in its chief characteristics to internationally accepted norms. In practice, this involved the introduction of a VAT and excise taxes, schedular personal income taxes, a profit tax to replace confiscatory profit taking from the enterprise sector, and the conversion of nontariff trade barriers to ad valorem duties. Together with the liberalization of prices and the gradual introduction of a modern tax system, there has also been a retrenchment in the scope of activities traditionally financed by the state affecting, mainly, a broad range of consumer and producer subsidies, a process that has contributed to reduce distortions in the economy and has laid the basis for a more stable macroeconomy.

Nevertheless, much remains to be done in the period ahead. This paper has tried to identify some of the key challenges facing decision makers over the medium term, with particular reference to the policy choices and institutional developments that must underpin the implementation of fiscal policy.

Key elements of the unfinished agenda on the revenue side include the following.

- The basic legal tax provisions remain embodied in a collection of legislative acts, presidential decrees, and government resolutions put together with no attempt at consistency or administrative simplicity. Furthermore, these are subject to frequent and unpredictable changes; for example, 24 different amended versions of the VAT and profit tax laws were promulgated in 1992–95. While the prospective adoption of a tax code should go a long way toward coherence and predictability in Russia's tax legislation, it will not, in and of itself, be effective without parallel improvements in other areas.

- The fiscal relationship between the federal government and the subjects of the federation needs to be clarified. Lack of clarity in this area has allowed the regional and local authorities to introduce many new taxes not envisaged in the tax legislation and has contributed to the general weakening of the tax-compliance environment. In the process, the system of intergovernmental fiscal relations has been undermined, as evidenced by the growing number of regions entering into "special" fiscal regimes with the federal government (involving, for instance, the remittance to the federal budget of a smaller VAT share from the region than called for in the law) or "single channel" agreements (which bypass revenue-sharing formulas altogether), thus introducing an element of arbitrariness in the intergovernmental relations that the system of fiscal federalism was initially intended to prevent.

- The widespread use of tax exemptions, often with the declared aim of "supporting key sectors of the economy" or "boosting economic activity," but more often reflecting lobbying efforts by key constituencies representing various vested interests, has been one of the main rea-

---

[72]Kornai (1992, p. 5).

sons for the decline in revenues. No attempts have been made to keep track of all exemptions in place or, in the context of preparation of the budget, to estimate the implied revenue loss and to examine their macroeconomic impact. There is no tax for which there is not some form of exemption, no sector of the economy that has not sought and obtained some form of tax relief; thus tax privileges have become the rule rather than the exception. In the context of tight budgets brought about by the need to bring inflation under control, discretionary recourse to exemptions has made the task of fiscal adjustment more difficult than would otherwise have been necessary, imposing severe constraints on the permissible level of government expenditures and, more generally, undermining public support for economic reform.

- The large increase in the number of taxpayers and the shift in economic activity from the enterprise sector to the emerging private economy (registered or otherwise) has imposed a heavy burden on the administrative capacities of the authorities and complicated tax collection more generally. Tax administration needs to move away from the present system—characterized by large-scale involvement of tax officials in routine functions associated with reporting by taxpayers—to a system guided by the application of internationally accepted principles, such as self-assessment and voluntary compliance. This needs to be supported by a credible system of penalties and fines to discourage noncompliance, efforts to improve coordination between the center and the regional tax authorities, closer monitoring of tax exemptions, the creation of a master file of registered taxpayers that would facilitate the tasks of audit and control, and the creation of a streamlined accounting framework with simpler forms and procedures to encourage taxpayers to fulfill tax obligations. Of critical importance in all of this is the need for the state to earn the confidence of the population that it will use these resources well and in the interests of the public at large and not to preserve the privileges of lobby or interest groups. Without this, tax evasion and noncompliance could become a permanent feature of Russia's fiscal environment, with disturbing implications for market reforms in general, popular support for them, and, ultimately, the prospects for a recovery of economic growth.

On the expenditure side, key elements of the unfinished agenda include the following.

- The chief priority on the expenditure side is to move away from the pervasive system of ex-

penditure sequestration used in the execution of the budget when faced with revenue shortfalls. As presently applied in Russia, sequestration has introduced a high degree of arbitrariness in the spending process. The spending authorizations included in the budget have become no more than a loose framework providing spending units a rough indication of the maximum level of resources that could potentially become available in the course of the fiscal year. This, inevitably, has introduced considerable uncertainty in their operations, making it difficult to plan and prioritize and focusing the attention of managers in these units on finding ways to lobby the government to maintain a certain flow of financing, at least large enough to pay wages. Sequestration has given rise to situations where individual spending units have unilaterally implemented decisions (for example, wage increases in the military) not contemplated in the budget that, after the event, the government has had to validate on the margins of the budget law—for instance, by granting guarantees to the spending units for short-term borrowing from the banking system. Sequestration has also contributed to the growth of arrears, including in the payment of taxes to the budget. It has thus severely undermined the credibility of the budget as an instrument of fiscal policy and of the government as the architect of that policy.

Sequestration has also often shielded the government and parliament from making difficult policy choices in a number of areas. It has sharply limited the ability of the government to monitor the structure of expenditure over time and hence to prevent abuses and the misallocation of scarce resources by individual spending units. There is no alternative, over the medium term, to the elaboration and execution of a budget that is based on realistic macroeconomic assumptions and that economic agents come to recognize as the legal framework within which the state will carry out its responsibilities as the economy's main intermediary of financial resources.

- A credible budget becomes an urgent priority in the context of a country where the scope for an additional compression of expenditures has probably been exhausted and where there are a number of identified areas where spending pressures will remain over the medium term. These include
  — interest payments, given the rapid accumulation of public debt and the use of market-based debt instruments to finance fiscal deficits;

— wages, to narrow the gap with respect to the private sector and as various hidden subsidies at the enterprise level continue to be eliminated;

— capital spending, to stem further deterioration of the country's physical infrastructure and of the health and education systems;

— environmental cleanup; and, more generally,

— institution-building, including support for improvements in the judicial area and institutions created in the context of a market economy.

Priority reforms in the area of social protection include the following.

• The link between the value of pensions and increases in the cost of living needs to be strengthened. This would involve a closer correlation between regional pension levels and the regional cost of living and, in particular, a shift of the minimum pension to the level of the minimum subsistence level.

• The Pension Fund's revenue base should be improved by including in-kind benefits in the wage base and eliminating a number of exemptions that, with growing arrears in the payment of contributions, have contributed to significantly reduce the effective contribution rate.

• The burden of financing pensions should be distributed more equitably between employers and employees by increasing the contribution rate of the latter while reducing that of the former.

• The functions of the Pension Fund and the Ministry of Labor and Social Development in administering the pension system should be integrated and the jurisdiction over the various social funds clarified. These reforms should also unify the collection of contributions by the various funds.

• The value of benefits should be delinked from the level of the minimum wage, moving to a system involving a greater degree of targeting than at present.

Concerted government action in addressing these challenges should go a long way toward creating a stable macroeconomic environment in Russia, characterized by the rule of law and broad acceptance by the government and the public of the patterns of governance and economic behavior increasingly evident in the developed world. In the absence of such actions, public support for market reforms in general is likely to remain weak or weaken further, confidence in the future is likely to be undermined, the achievement of political stability is likely to remain a distant goal, and an environment conducive to growth is unlikely to emerge. In the absence of growth, a significant improvement in the standard of living of the population is also likely to be postponed. This would be a loss not only for Russia, a country that is so richly endowed with natural and human capital resources, but also for the international community, given the ongoing processes of global integration and the potential contributions that Russia could make to the world economy.

VII Bibliography

Alesina, Alberto, 1998, "The Political Economy of Macroeconomic Stabilizations and Income Inequality: Myths and Reality," in *Income Distribution and High-Quality Growth*," ed. by Vito Tanzi and Ke-young Chu (Cambridge, Massachusetts: MIT Press).

_____, and Roberto Perotti, 1995, "The Political Economy of Budget Deficits," *Staff Papers,* International Monetary Fund, Vol. 42 (March), p. 1–31.

Alexashenko, Sergei, 1992, "The Collapse of the Soviet Fiscal System: What Should Be Done?" Bank of Finland (Helsinki).

_____, 1993, "Macroeconomic Stabilization in the Former Soviet Republics: Dream or Reality?" in *Economic Consequences of the Soviet Disintegration,* ed. by John Williamson (Washington: Institute for International Economics).

Åslund, Anders, 1994, "Russia's Success Story," *Foreign Affairs,* Vol. 73 (September–October), pp. 58–71.

_____, 1995, *How Russia Became a Market Economy* (Washington: Brookings Institution).

Barbone, Luca, and Domenico Marchetti, Jr., 1995, "Transition and the Fiscal Crisis in Central Europe," *Economics of Transition,* Vol. 3 (March), pp. 59–74.

Cheasty, Adrienne, and Jeffrey M. Davis, 1996, "Fiscal Transition in Countries of the Former Soviet Union: An Interim Assessment," IMF Working Paper 96/61 (Washington: International Monetary Fund).

Chu, Ke-young, and Gerd Schwartz, 1994, "Output Decline and Government Expenditures in European Transition Economies," IMF Working Paper 94/68 (Washington: International Monetary Fund).

Chu, Ke-young, and Sanjeev Gupta, 1996, "Social Protection in Transition Countries: Emerging Issues," IMF Paper on Policy Analysis and Assessment 96/5 (Washington: International Monetary Fund).

Christensen, Benedicte Vibe, 1994, *The Russian Federation in Transition: External Developments,* IMF Occasional Paper 111 (Washington: International Monetary Fund).

Citrin, Daniel A., and Ashok K. Lahiri, 1995, eds., *Policy Experiences and Issues in the Baltics, Russia, and Other Countries of the Former Soviet Union,* IMF Occasional Paper 133 (Washington: International Monetary Fund).

Corden, Max W., 1989, "Macroeconomic Adjustment in Developing Countries," *World Bank Research Observer,* Vol. 4 (January), pp. 51–64.

Craig, Jon, John Norregaard, and George Tsibouris, 1997, "Russian Federation," in *Fiscal Federalism in Theory and Practice,* ed. by Teresa Ter-Minassian (Washington: International Monetary Fund).

Craig, R. Sean, and Catherine L. Mann, 1992, "Fiscal Implications of the Transition from Planned to Market Economy," International Finance Discussion Paper 424 (Washington: Board of Governors of the Federal Reserve System).

Ebrill, Liam P., and others, 1994, *Poland: The Path to a Market Economy,* IMF Occasional Paper 113 (Washington: International Monetary Fund).

Etzioni, Amitai, 1988, *The Moral Dimension: Toward a New Economics* (New York: Free Press).

Gavrilenkov, Evgeny, and Vincent Koen, 1995, "How Large Was the Output Collapse in Russia? Alternative Estimates and Welfare Implications," *Staff Studies for the World Economic Outlook,* World Economic and Financial Surveys (Washington: International Monetary Fund).

Gray, Dale F., "Evaluation of Taxes and Revenues from the Energy Sector in the Baltics, Russia, and Other Former Soviet Union Countries," IMF Working Paper (Washington: International Monetary Fund, forthcoming).

Illarionov, A., 1995, "Attempts to Carry Out Policies of Financial Stabilization in the U.S.S.R. and Russia," *Voprosy Ekonomiki,* No. 7, pp. 4–37.

International Monetary Fund, European I Department, 1994, "Factors Underlying the Weakening Performance of Tax Revenues," IMF Working Paper 94/104 (Washington).

_____, Fiscal Affairs Department, 1995, *Unproductive Public Expenditures: A Pragmatic Approach to Policy Analysis,* IMF Pamphlet Series 48 (Washington).

_____, Fiscal Affairs Department, Expenditure Policy Division, 1995, "Social Safety Nets for Economic Transition: Options and Recent Experiences," IMF Paper on Policy Analysis and Assessment 95/3 (Washington).

_____, World Bank, Organization for Economic Cooperation and Development, and European Bank for Reconstruction and Development, 1991, *A Study of the Soviet Economy,* 3 vols. (Paris).

Klugman, Jeni, ed., 1997, *Poverty in Russia* (Washngton: World Bank).

Koen, Vincent, and Steven Phillips, 1993, *Price Liberalization in Russia: Behavior of Prices, Household Incomes, and Consumption During the First Year,* IMF Occasional Paper 104 (Washington: International Monetary Fund).

Kornai, János, 1986, "The Soft Budget Constraint," *Kyklos,* Vol. 39 (No. 1), pp. 3–30.

———, 1992, "The Postsocialist Transition and the State: Reflections in the Light of Hungarian Fiscal Problems," *American Economic Review, Papers and Proceedings,* Vol. 82 (May), pp. 1–21.

Kovalev, S., 1997, "Russia After Chechnya," *New York Review of Books,* Vol. 44, No. 12, July 17, pp. 27–31.

Lambeth, Benjamin S., 1995, "Russia's Wounded Military," *Foreign Affairs,* Vol. 74 (March–April), pp. 86–98.

Landell-Mills, Pierre, and Ismail Serageldin, 1991, "Governance and the Development Process," *Finance & Development* (September), pp. 14–17.

Le Houerou, Philippe, Elana Gold, and Stanislav Katash, 1994, "Budget Coverage and Government Finance in the Russian Federation," Internal Discussion Paper, Report No. IDP-137, Europe and Central Asia Region (Washington: World Bank).

Lipton, David, and Jeffrey D. Sachs, 1992, "Prospects for Russia's Economic Reforms," *Brookings Papers in Economic Activity: 2,* pp. 213–83.

Lopez-Claros, Augusto, 1993, "The International Monetary Fund's Approach to Macroeconomic Adjustment," *Money and Credit,* Central Bank of Russia (February) (in Russian).

———, 1994, "Nekotorie Prioritety Ekonomicheskikh Reform v Rossii v 1990-e Gody," *Znamya* (December), pp. 168–72.

Maret, Xavier, and Gerd Schwartz, 1993, "Poland: The Social Safety Net During the Transition," IMF Working Paper 93/42 (Washington: International Monetary Fund).

Matlock, Jack F., Jr., 1996, "Dealing with a Russia in Turmoil," *Foreign Affairs,* Vol. 75 (May–June), pp. 38–51.

McFaul, Michael, 1995, "Why Russia's Politics Matter," *Foreign Affairs,* Vol. 74 (January-February), pp. 87–99.

Mikhalev, Vladimir, 1996, "Social Security in Russia Under Economic Transformation," *Europe-Asia Studies,* Vol. 48 (January), pp. 5–25.

Plessix Gray, Francine du, 1989, *Soviet Women: Walking the Tightrope* (New York: Doubleday).

Remmick, David, 1997, "Can Russia Change?" *Foreign Affairs,* Vol. 76 (January–February), pp. 35–49.

Sachs, Jeffrey D., and Katharina Pistor, eds., 1997, *The Rule of Law and Economic Reform in Russia* (Boulder, Colorado: Westview Press).

Secretaría General para la Seguridad Social, 1996, "La Seguridad Social en el Umbral del Siglo XXI," *Estudio Económico-Actuarial* (Madrid: Centro de Publicaciones, Ministerio de Trabajo y Seguridad Social).

Summers, Lawrence H., and Vinod Thomas, 1993, "Recent Lessons of Development," *World Bank Research Observer,* Vol. 8 (July), pp. 241–54.

Tanzi, Vito, ed., 1992, *Fiscal Policies in Economies in Transition* (Washington: International Monetary Fund).

———, 1993a, "The Budget Deficit in Transition," *Staff Papers,* International Monetary Fund, Vol. 40 (September), pp. 697–707.

———, 1993b, "Fiscal Policy and the Economic Restructuring of Economies in Transition," IMF Working Paper 93/22 (Washington: International Monetary Fund).

———, ed., 1993c, *Transition to Market: Studies in Fiscal Reform* (Washington: International Monetary Fund).

———, 1997, "The Changing Role of the State in the Economy: A Historical Perspective," IMF Working Paper 97/114 (Washington: International Monetary Fund).

United Nations Children's Fund, International Child Development Centre, *Central and Eastern Europe in Transition: Public Policy and Social Conditions,* Regional Monitoring Reports, November 1993, August 1994, August 1995, and February 1997 (Florence).

Wallich, Christine I., 1992, "Fiscal Decentralization: Intergovernmental Relations in Russia," Studies of Eco-nomies in Transformation (Washington: World Bank).

Williamson, John, 1991, "Current Issues in Transition Economics," in *International Financial Policy: Essays in Honor of Jacques J. Polak,* ed. by Jacob A. Frenkel and Morris Goldstein (Washington: International Monetary Fund and Netherlands Bank).

Wolf, Thomas A., 1985, "Economic Stabilization in Planned Economies," *Staff Papers,* International Monetary Fund, Vol. 32 (March), pp. 78–131.

———, 1990a, "Macroeconomic Adjustment and Reform in Planned Economies," IMF Working Paper 90/27 (Washington: International Monetary Fund).

———, 1990b, "Reform, Inflation, and Adjustment in Planned Economies," *Finance & Development* (March), pp. 2–5.

———, 1994, "Currency Arrangements in Countries of the Former Ruble Area and Conditions for Sound Monetary Policy," IMF Paper on Policy Analysis and Assessment 94/15 (Washington: International Monetary Fund).

World Bank, Country Operations Division II, Europe and Central Asia Region, 1995a, *Russian Federation: Towards Medium-Term Viability* (Washington).

———, Human Resources Division, Europe and Central Asia Country Department III, 1995b, *Poverty in Russia: An Assessment* (Washington).

———, 1996, *Fiscal Management in Russia* (Washington).

Recent Occasional Papers of the International Monetary Fund

155. Fiscal Policy Issues During the Transition in Russia, by Augusto Lopez-Claros and Sergei V. Alexashenko. 1998.

154. Credibility Without Rules? Monetary Frameworks in the Post–Bretton Woods Era, by Carlo Cottarelli and Curzio Giannini. 1997.

153. Pension Regimes and Saving, by G.A. Mackenzie, Philip Gerson, and Alfredo Cuevas. 1997.

152. Hong Kong, China: Growth, Structural Change, and Economic Stability During the Transition, by John Dodsworth and Dubravko Mihaljek. 1997.

151. Currency Board Arrangements: Issues and Experiences, by a staff team led by Tomás J.T. Baliño and Charles Enoch. 1997.

150. Kuwait: From Reconstruction to Accumulation for Future Generations, by Nigel Andrew Chalk, Mohamed A. El-Erian, Susan J. Fennell, Alexei P. Kireyev, and John F. Wison. 1997.

149. The Composition of Fiscal Adjustment and Growth: Lessons from Fiscal Reforms in Eight Economies, by G.A. Mackenzie, David W.H. Orsmond, and Philip R. Gerson. 1997.

148. Nigeria: Experience with Structural Adjustment, by Gary Moser, Scott Rogers, and Reinold van Til, with Robin Kibuka and Inutu Lukonga. 1997.

147. Aging Populations and Public Pension Schemes, by Sheetal K. Chand and Albert Jaeger. 1996.

146. Thailand: The Road to Sustained Growth, by Kalpana Kochhar, Louis Dicks-Mireaux, Balazs Horvath, Mauro Mecagni, Erik Offerdal, and Jianping Zhou. 1996.

145. Exchange Rate Movements and Their Impact on Trade and Investment in the APEC Region, by Takatoshi Ito, Peter Isard, Steven Symansky, and Tamim Bayoumi. 1996.

144. National Bank of Poland: The Road to Indirect Instruments, by Piero Ugolini. 1996.

143. Adjustment for Growth: The African Experience, by Michael T. Hadjimichael, Michael Nowak, Robert Sharer, and Amor Tahari. 1996.

142. Quasi-Fiscal Operations of Public Financial Institutions, by G.A. Mackenzie and Peter Stella. 1996.

141. Monetary and Exchange System Reforms in China: An Experiment in Gradualism, by Hassanali Mehran, Marc Quintyn, Tom Nordman, and Bernard Laurens. 1996.

140. Government Reform in New Zealand, by Graham C. Scott. 1996.

139. Reinvigorating Growth in Developing Countries: Lessons from Adjustment Policies in Eight Economies, by David Goldsbrough, Sharmini Coorey, Louis Dicks-Mireaux, Balazs Horvath, Kalpana Kochhar, Mauro Mecagni, Erik Offerdal, and Jianping Zhou. 1996.

138. Aftermath of the CFA Franc Devaluation, by Jean A.P. Clément, with Johannes Mueller, Stéphane Cossé, and Jean Le Dem. 1996.

137. The Lao People's Democratic Republic: Systemic Transformation and Adjustment, edited by Ichiro Otani and Chi Do Pham. 1996.

136. Jordan: Strategy for Adjustment and Growth, edited by Edouard Maciejewski and Ahsan Mansur. 1996.

135. Vietnam: Transition to a Market Economy, by John R. Dodsworth, Erich Spitäller, Michael Braulke, Keon Hyok Lee, Kenneth Miranda, Christian Mulder, Hisanobu Shishido, and Krishna Srinivasan. 1996.

134. India: Economic Reform and Growth, by Ajai Chopra, Charles Collyns, Richard Hemming, and Karen Parker with Woosik Chu and Oliver Fratzscher. 1995.

133. Policy Experiences and Issues in the Baltics, Russia, and Other Countries of the Former Soviet Union, edited by Daniel A. Citrin and Ashok K. Lahiri. 1995.

132. Financial Fragilities in Latin America: The 1980s and 1990s, by Liliana Rojas-Suárez and Steven R. Weisbrod. 1995.

131. Capital Account Convertibility: Review of Experience and Implications for IMF Policies, by staff teams headed by Peter J. Quirk and Owen Evans. 1995.

130. Challenges to the Swedish Welfare State, by Desmond Lachman, Adam Bennett, John H. Green, Robert Hagemann, and Ramana Ramaswamy. 1995.

129. IMF Conditionality: Experience Under Stand-By and Extended Arrangements. Part II: Background Papers. Susan Schadler, Editor, with Adam Bennett, Maria Carkovic, Louis Dicks-Mireaux, Mauro Mecagni, James H.J. Morsink, and Miguel A. Savastano. 1995.

128. IMF Conditionality: Experience Under Stand-By and Extended Arrangements. Part I: Key Issues and Findings, by Susan Schadler, Adam Bennett, Maria Carkovic, Louis Dicks-Mireaux, Mauro Mecagni, James H.J. Morsink, and Miguel A. Savastano. 1995.

127. Road Maps of the Transition: The Baltics, the Czech Republic, Hungary, and Russia, by Biswajit Banerjee, Vincent Koen, Thomas Krueger, Mark S. Lutz, Michael Marrese, and Tapio O. Saavalainen. 1995.

126. The Adoption of Indirect Instruments of Monetary Policy, by a staff team headed by William E. Alexander, Tomás J.T. Baliño, and Charles Enoch. 1995.

125. United Germany: The First Five Years—Performance and Policy Issues, by Robert Corker, Robert A. Feldman, Karl Habermeier, Hari Vittas, and Tessa van der Willigen. 1995.

124. Saving Behavior and the Asset Price "Bubble" in Japan: Analytical Studies, edited by Ulrich Baumgartner and Guy Meredith. 1995.

123. Comprehensive Tax Reform: The Colombian Experience, edited by Parthasarathi Shome. 1995.

122. Capital Flows in the APEC Region, edited by Mohsin S. Khan and Carmen M. Reinhart. 1995.

121. Uganda: Adjustment with Growth, 1987–94, by Robert L. Sharer, Hema R. De Zoysa, and Calvin A. McDonald. 1995.

120. Economic Dislocation and Recovery in Lebanon, by Sena Eken, Paul Cashin, S. Nuri Erbas, Jose Martelino, and Adnan Mazarei. 1995.

119. Singapore: A Case Study in Rapid Development, edited by Kenneth Bercuson with a staff team comprising Robert G. Carling, Aasim M. Husain, Thomas Rumbaugh, and Rachel van Elkan. 1995.

118. Sub-Saharan Africa: Growth, Savings, and Investment, by Michael T. Hadjimichael, Dhaneshwar Ghura, Martin Mühleisen, Roger Nord, and E. Murat Uçer. 1995.

117. Resilience and Growth Through Sustained Adjustment: The Moroccan Experience, by Saleh M. Nsouli, Sena Eken, Klaus Enders, Van-Can Thai, Jörg Decressin, and Filippo Cartiglia, with Janet Bungay. 1995.

116. Improving the International Monetary System: Constraints and Possibilities, by Michael Mussa, Morris Goldstein, Peter B. Clark, Donald J. Mathieson, and Tamim Bayoumi. 1994.

115. Exchange Rates and Economic Fundamentals: A Framework for Analysis, by Peter B. Clark, Leonardo Bartolini, Tamim Bayoumi, and Steven Symansky. 1994.

114. Economic Reform in China: A New Phase, by Wanda Tseng, Hoe Ee Khor, Kalpana Kochhar, Dubravko Mihaljek, and David Burton. 1994.

113. Poland: The Path to a Market Economy, by Liam P. Ebrill, Ajai Chopra, Charalambos Christofides, Paul Mylonas, Inci Otker, and Gerd Schwartz. 1994.

112. The Behavior of Non-Oil Commodity Prices, by Eduardo Borensztein, Mohsin S. Khan, Carmen M. Reinhart, and Peter Wickham. 1994.

111. The Russian Federation in Transition: External Developments, by Benedicte Vibe Christensen. 1994.

110. Limiting Central Bank Credit to the Government: Theory and Practice, by Carlo Cottarelli. 1993.

109. The Path to Convertibility and Growth: The Tunisian Experience, by Saleh M. Nsouli, Sena Eken, Paul Duran, Gerwin Bell, and Zühtü Yücelik. 1993.

108. Recent Experiences with Surges in Capital Inflows, by Susan Schadler, Maria Carkovic, Adam Bennett, and Robert Kahn. 1993.

Note: For information on the title and availability of Occasional Papers not listed, please consult the IMF Publications Catalog or contact IMF Publication Services.